Don't Let Your Film Die

How to Plan a Successful Launch Without Going Broke

by

Elliott Kanbar

Author of *You Finally Finished Your Film. Now What?*

© 2015 by Elliott Kanbar

All Rights Reserved

No part of this publication may be reproduced, stored in a retrieval system, or transmitted in any form or by any means, electronic, mechanical, photocopying, recording or otherwise, without prior permission in writing from the publisher, except in the case of brief quotations in critical articles and reviews. Without limiting the rights under copyright reserved above, no part of this publication may be reproduced, stored in or introduced into a retrieval system, or transmitted, in any form, or by any means (electronic, mechanical, photocopying, recording, or otherwise), without the prior written permission of the publisher of the book. The scanning, uploading, and distribution of this book via the Internet or any other means without the permission of the publisher is illegal and punishable by law. Please purchase only authorized electronic editions, and do not participate in or encourage electronic piracy of copyrighted materials. Your support of the author's rights is appreciated.

Council Oak Books
San Francisco & Oakland
www.counciloakbooks.com

ISBN 069244212X
EAN 9780692442128
Library of Congress Control Number: 2015907983
Council Oak Books, San Francisco & Oakland, CA
Printed in the United States of America

Table of Contents

Introduction		5
Chapter 1	Reality Checks—Face Them Now	9
Chapter 2	10 Rules for Successful Film Distribution	13
Chapter 3	Your Website Is Your Store—Do It Right	17
Chapter 4	IMDb—A Vital Listing	23
Chapter 5	Financing—A Big Hurdle	29
Chapter 6	Crowdfunding—A Viable Option	33
Chapter 7	Hiring a Publicist—A Key Player	39
Chapter 8	DIY Press Releases—It's Easy	45
Chapter 9	Finding a Distributor—Who Knows? You May Get Lucky	49
Chapter 10	National Distribution—Is It Still Worth Doing?	53
Chapter 11	Foreign Sales—A Rich Market	63
Chapter 12	DVD Sales—Still Alive and Kicking	71

Chapter 13	Cable Video On Demand—Better Days Are Coming	77
Chapter 14	Four-Walling—Don't Dismiss It	83
Chapter 15	Streaming—It's the Future	87
Chapter 16	Facebook—One Billion Users and Counting	93
Chapter 17	Google AdWords—The #1 Search Engine	97
Chapter 18	LinkedIn—More Than a Job-Hunting Site	103
Chapter 19	Trailers—Your Film's Resume	107
Chapter 20	Film Festivals—Are They Worth the Cost?	111
Chapter 21	Major Film Markets—Buyers and Sellers Wheeling and Dealing	119
Chapter 22	Qualifying for an Oscar—Why Not?	123
Chapter 23	Trade Publications—Read Them	129
Chapter 24	Film Equipment—Don't Overspend	135
Chapter 25	Terms & Definitions	139
INDEX		145

Introduction

> "We don't make movies to make money; we make money to make movies."
>
> —Walt Disney

Do not read this book if

- You've sold your film for big bucks to an investor.

- You've found a well-connected distributor who promised to make you rich and famous.

- You've given up on your film and are willing to let it die.

If you've answered negatively to any of the above, then this book will help point you in the right direction to successfully and economically launch your film.

Don't Let Your Film Die covers a wide range of topics but focuses primarily on how to generate the most income from your film. When the film is finally completed and the celebrations are over, reality usually sets in. You'll quickly come to the painful realization that your film has got to make money—money to pay off your investors, money to pay off your loans, and enough left over to finance your next film.

There are six major sources of income for most indie films:

1. Theatrical. This still represents the heart and soul of film distribution. A theatrical run in either New York or Los Angeles will give your film the ultimate exposure. But, more importantly, a theatrical run will result in reviews, hopefully good ones. See Chapters 10 and 14.

2. Digital Platforms. There are hundreds of them out there and more popping up each day. The five I favor are Netflix, Amazon, iTunes, Hulu, and Google Play. There are two important advantages to having your film included on these digital platforms: they are global and they will often list your film for a long stretch of time, sometimes for months. Most of these platforms sell DVDs as well as stream films. See Chapter 15.

3. DVD Sales. True, it's a diminishing source of income. But people are still buying DVDs because they are handy to carry, easy to use, perfect on vacations, and make great gifts. DVDs are slowly vanishing from retail store shelves, but schools, colleges, and libraries still buy DVDs. See Chapter 12.

4. Cable Video On Demand. These are the hardest outlets for indie films to crack. Cable stations tend to favor the big Hollywood blockbusters. But this is changing. Cable stations are beginning to add indie films to their lineups because they want to attract new subscribers and retain the subscribers they already have. The big ones are Comcast, Time Warner, Cablevision, and Cox. See Chapter 13.

5. Foreign Sales. Most foreign countries have still not felt the full impact of the digital platforms and the streaming of films. Therefore, they are still buying and booking films for theatrical runs. You may be able to earn substantial income working through a competent and transparent international sales agent. If your film

is good enough, you can pre-sell it and cover your post-production costs. See Chapter 11.

6. Website Sales. In addition to all of the above, your website should serve as your "store" to sell DVDs of your film. Remember, your website reaches a global audience. How will people know about your film? That's why you need a successful theatrical run and good reviews. See Chapter 3.

7. TV Sales. Could be your most lucrative source of income.

A key factor to making money from your film is to keep your costs low. For this reason, this book includes a chapter on filmmaking equipment. Too often I've seen filmmakers spend tons of money on the latest cameras and every conceivable gadget. It may make them feel more professional, but the latest equipment will never be more important than telling a good story, building a well-constructed plot, and casting talented actors. See Chapter 24.

I confess that I am obsessed with lists. There are plenty of them in my book because they are a very efficient way to highlight points I want to emphasize. I also feel that a list will make it much easier to digest what is often some very dense stuff.

I am assuming that most of you reading this book have opted to self-distribute. In recent years I have also observed filmmakers preferring to self-distribute even though their films caught the eye of a few good distributors. There are persuasive reasons to self-distribute: you retain rights to your film, you maximize income, and you control your costs. However, you should be aware of the following:

• You will have to spend money to self-distribute. You will avoid suicidal stress if you fold these expenses into your filmmaking budget. They should not be considered "extra" expenses, and you should not let them take you by surprise.

• Promoting and marketing your film are your responsibilities. The book includes many chapters on strategies for doing so without breaking your budget.

This book was not intended to be read from cover to cover (although I would be flattered if you did). Each chapter was written to stand on its own. Pick and choose the chapters that are most meaningful for you.

Lastly, I welcome comments, suggestions, case histories, and even criticism. Please contact me either by mail, email, or phone.

Elliott Kanbar
c/o Council Oak Books
2100 Jackson Street
San Francisco, CA 94115
eskanbar@aol.com
212-628-4990

Chapter 1
Reality Checks—Face Them Now

> "My three Ps: passion, patience, perseverance. You've got to have these if you're going to be a filmmaker."
>
> —Robert Wise

After months and maybe years of work, after begging for money from every living relative and friend, after maxing your credit cards, and after existing on day-old bread and water, you finally finished your film.

Now what?

Reality sets in. It's time to get down to earth and realize what's happening out there, and how the film industry has changed dramatically in just the past five years. Know this before taking the next step:

• Distributors, with few exceptions, are not paying big bucks for films. If you do not have a successful track record or a few well-known actors in your film, your chances of getting a distributor (with a hefty advance) are next to nil. Be very wary of a distributor deal with no (or very little) advance payment. You may be tying up your film for years and have nothing to show for it.

• If you do receive an advance, consider it the only income you'll ever see. Ever hear of "creative accounting?" An advance is a payment on projected sales. Companies have all kinds of ways of massaging the numbers so that, even after you've met that projection, it will seem as if they never owe you any more.

• With the development of inexpensive cameras and post-production software, there is a glut of films all searching for screen space. It's estimated that over 50,000 indie films will be completed in 2015. Be prepared for the competition.

• In all likelihood, the theatrical release will not pay back your investment. Consider the theatrical release a marketing expense and include it in your total budget.

• Realize that people are now watching films many different ways—at home, on computers, on tablets, even on cellphones. Develop your marketing plan with this in mind.

• Be prepared to do all the promoting and marketing of your film. Getting your film on a digital platform like iTunes, Netflix, or Amazon is only the beginning. These companies will do very little (if anything) to promote your film.

• Do not consider self-distributing your film as a sign of failure. It's the way most filmmakers (including some big honchos) are distributing their films these days.

• Be realistic about film festivals. They are fine for getting some exposure and evaluating audience reactions to your film. But the days when you fly back home from a festival with a big fat check in your pocket are almost over.

• There are fewer art house theaters. In New York alone, we've lost such icons as the Thalia, Regency, Baronet, Coronet,

Beekman, Sutton, Carnegie Hall Cinema, Art, Fifth Avenue Cinema, Greenwich, Plaza, and Olympia. A shortage of acceptable venues for indie films is a major factor why distributors are not hooking up with more filmmakers.

Peter Broderick, a highly regarded film consultant, said the following at the Vancouver International Film Festival: "It's time filmmakers took more control of the distribution of their films. The old distribution model is broken. Filmmakers should try and retain as many rights of their work as they can. Filmmakers are either finding themselves blocked out from conventional distribution channels or stuck in lousy distribution deals where they see little or no return."

Chapter 2
10 Rules for Successful Film Distribution

"It's all just one film to me. Just different chapters."

—Robert Altman

There are tons of books and articles written on how to successfully distribute a film. And there are hundreds of consultants and brainy film mavens who argue about the best strategies at film festivals. Trying to figure out the best way to approach this task can unnerve even the hardiest soul.

After 42 years in the film business, mentoring and assisting young filmmakers, I've come up with 10 rules which, if followed, will help you to successfully and economically launch your film.

Rule #1: Open your film in a highly regarded theater in New York for a minimum of one week. Elliott Grove, a respected film journalist, said it best at the recent Raindance Film Festival: "Why do a theatrical release? The biggest asset is that a theatrical release guarantees critical notices in all the main newspapers in the country it has been released. This brings the film to the public's attention and creates increased value for the film when it is available in other formats such as DVD or online streaming through portals like Netflix."

Rule #2: Don't stint on getting a publicist who is experienced in the film business. However, you can keep the cost down by having the publicist focus on three areas: contacting the film critics, writing and mailing press releases, and compiling and distributing production notes.

Rule #3: Set up a campaign for marketing the film on the major digital platforms (Netflix, Amazon, iTunes, Hulu, and Google Play) and cable Video On Demand stations (Comcast, Cablevision, Time Warner, and Cox). But do this only after you've complied with Rule #1 and Rule #2.

Rule #4: Promote your film on the search engines (Google, Bing, and Yahoo) and the social networks (Facebook & Twitter).

Rule #5: Make sure your film is feature length. 70 minutes is the minimum. Many publications will not review a film that is under 60 minutes.

Rule #6: Adhere to the 50/50 percentages. Allocate 50 percent of your budget for producing the film and 50 percent for marketing and promoting your film.

Rule #7: Don't edit your own film. There's no way you can be objective. Many potentially good films have been ruined by bad editing.

Rule #8: Don't rush to distribute your film nationally. Consider doing this only after your film has had a successful run in New York and/or Los Angeles. The digital platforms (see Rule # 3) do a great jobs reaching both a national and a global audience.

Rule #9: Don't overspend on filmmaking equipment. A key to success is to keep your costs very low. Film schools are now teaching courses on how to make feature-length films on a cell phone.

Rule #10: I am a cost-cutter in every way possible. However, use experienced film professionals to do the following jobs: (a) make still photographs and videos during filming, (b) design the website, and (c) design the poster.

Chapter 3
Your Website Is Your Store—Do It Right

> "If I ever was stranded on a desert island there would be three things I'd need: food, shelter, and a grip."
>
> —George C. Scott

Creating an effective, well-designed website is the very first step in successfully launching your film. The website is your store that can promote your film to the entire world. It's your best shot to tell everyone where they can stream or download your film, and where they can buy DVDs. Since these are great sources for generating income, you want to make sure your website is well-designed.

Here's why:

• It gives moviegoers vital information about your film.

• You'll have the opportunity to include a trailer.

• It will make you discoverable on search engines, especially Google.

• It may attract distributors, exhibitors, and investors.

• You can inform viewers where the film will be opening, where they can buy DVDs, and where it can be downloaded and/or streamed.

• You can include reviews, favorable press releases, and awards.

There are many companies offering to design your website inexpensively. Do not succumb to deals that sound too good to be true. Cheap is cheap. Unless you are a very competent computer geek, hire a professional website designer to do the job. The website will become the film's window to the entire world. Don't stint on this expense.

Choosing the right website designer can be a challenge. Here's what you should check before signing on:

• How long has the person been in the website designing business?

• Look at the designer's own website. It will give you an idea of the kind of work you can expect.

• Has the designer created any websites for other films? If so, ask to see them.

• Determine how long the designer will need to complete the job.

• Ensure that the designer is familiar with Search Engine Optimization (SEO).

• Ensure that the website will render well on all major mobile devices.

• Get a written agreement.

• And, lastly, check the price. Best to get a few proposals and compare prices.

Domain Name. Registering a domain name is your next step. Some may prefer to do so before designing the website. It could simply be the name of your film.com. For example, if the name of your film is "Breaking the Barrier," the domain name could be: www.breakingthebarrier.com. Choose the name carefully. It is the home address for your website. Once registered, it cannot be changed. You can only register a new name. Keep the name short so you can get matching usernames on Twitter, YouTube, and other social media outlets. Your website designer will register the name for you. There will be a cost, which will vary, depending on the number of years you specify for the domain name to be active.

WordPress. More than half of the websites on the Internet are running on WordPress. Your website designer should use WordPress. With WordPress you can easily make changes, add content, images, and videos. Your website will look more professional and will work more easily on the mobile devices.

Website Host. You will need a website host. The host "holds" your website and manages it. Once the host is on board, everyone in the world will be able to access and view the pages.

Here are some things to consider before selecting the host:

• How long has the company been in business? Stay away from newcomers or startups. Five years' experience is about right.

• Are they easily accessible? Ideally, you should have a contact person who can be reached by phone or e-mail.

• Do they have a 24/7 hotline to handle emergencies? They will happen.

• What is their monthly fee? Average should be around $5. Be wary if it's less.

• Do they have the ability to run WordPress?

• Can they provide enough storage to handle your files without additional cost?

• Will they provide an analysis of website traffic?

Writing the Website. The old saying "garbage in, garbage out" certainly applies to website design. It will be your responsibility to provide the website designer with compelling, well-written (and well-edited) content that gives visitors the information they need.

Here are the important features to be included:

• Basic film data: Running time, rating, language the film is in.

• Contact information: The contact person, company name, address, phone, and e-mail address.

• Synopsis: Minimum of 100 words, maximum 300 words. Write it with care and, if necessary, use a professional.

• Poster: Make sure the small print on the poster can be easily read. This may require designing a poster just for the website.

• Trailer: Keep it under 3 minutes.

• Cast, director, producers: Include a short bio of each principal person involved in making the film.

• Background: Short summary of how and why the film was made.

• Testimonials, reviews, awards, and appearances at festivals.

• Photos and video clips: Use only high-quality, relevant photos and clips. They should help explain the film and not be head shots of yourself or your associates.

• Embed in your website a blog, Facebook, Twitter, and Foursquare accounts, and invite viewers to post comments.

Final Words: Make sure you own and control the website, usernames, and passwords. Keep updating your website. Do not feel that once it's done, it's finished. The website should be a work in progress. And, finally, require the website designer to send you all the original graphics and program files. Don't pay the balance until you receive all this stuff, in case you want to change the host.

Chapter 4
IMDB—A Vital Listing

> "Photography is truth. Cinema is truth twenty-four times per second."
>
> —Jean-Luc Godard

The Internet Movie Database (IMDb) is an online database of information about films. As of January 18, 2015, IMDb listed 3,156,631 titles, and had 58 million registered users. It is an Alexa Top 50 site and probably the most frequently viewed site by viewers seeking information and data about films. It is thus vital that your film be listed on IMDb. However, only certain kinds of films qualify. (See below.)

The IMDb Page. Hopefully, many viewers will access your film on IMDb. Therefore, you will want to ensure that the information you provide is complete, clearly organized, and totally transparent. Since IMDb reaches a global audience, you'll want your film available for downloading and streaming on as many digital platforms as you can get. IMDb is a subsidiary of Amazon, so having your film listed on that platform is a must.

The IMDb film page includes the following information, some of which you provide, and some that will be added for you:

• The Score. It's what most people look at. More about this later. In addition to the IMDb score, the page includes ratings from Metascore and Metacritic.

- Reviews. The page includes reviews from film critics from around the world, and comments from registered users.

- Trailer. Essential. Have it produced by a professional, and keep it under 3 minutes.

- Videos and Photos. Have them relate to the film. Avoid personal shots and videos.

- Cast. List everyone of importance. The more, the better. Include a job title or short bio for each one.

- Synopsis. 200 words maximum. 100 words is ideal.

- Genre. Specify: drama, family, comedy, sci-fi, horror, etc.

- Motion Picture Rating (MPAA). If your film has been rated R, explain why: language, nudity, explicit sexual scenes.

- Parents' Guide. Self-explanatory.

- Details. List the following information: film's website, language, country, release date, and film locations.

- Credits. List all producers, the director, and the distributor.

- Technical Specs. Running time, color, aspect ratio, format.

- Trivia. Include interesting facts about the making of the film, some noteworthy quotes, and anything else of interest.

- Frequently Asked Questions (FAQs). If there are none, you can answer questions you feel many viewers might ask.

• User Comments. Encourage viewers to post comments about your film.

• Message Board. The "catch-all" section of the page.

Getting Your Film Listed on IMDb: The first step is to click "help" on the IMDb home page. To submit a new title, you'll have to complete the "New Title Submission Form." Every film submitted must be approved by the IMDb editors. Before submitting your film, you should be aware of these IMDb rules:

• IMDb provides a list of the type of titles they consider acceptable. Check this list to make sure your film title qualifies.

• With few exceptions, it should be a completed film.

• Provide links showing evidence of the film's theatrical release (must be multiple screenings, not just one showing), TV appearances, or screenings at qualifying film festivals. Evidence should be from a third party (such as an ad, review, or media write-up) and not from someone connected with the production of the film.

• For films that have not yet been released, IMDb requires contact information of the production, links to announcements in the media/trade publications, published interviews with key cast and/or crew members, casting notices, and evidence of development deals.

• IMDb defines a "qualifying festival" as one that does not accept every submission. The ratio of submitted films to accepted films should be at least 3:1.

• Your film must be of "general public interest." IMDb considers a film qualified if it has been (1) released in a cinema, (2) shown on TV, (3) released on video or the web or has prints available to the public, (4) listed in the catalog of an established retailer, (5) accepted and shown in a qualifying film festival, (6) produced by a well-known, established person, and (7) is widely talked about/referenced in the media or film community.

• Your chances are improved if you have a website for the film. In the absence of a website, IMDb will sometimes accept the following links: a newspaper article, press release, a festival schedule, or a library's online catalog. But in 2015, a website is essential.

• Providing the necessary documentation is your responsibility. IMDb will not assist in any way.

• IMDb is a subsidiary of Amazon. If you sign on for the Amazon Instant Video Program (which you should do), your film will automatically be included on IMDb.

The All-Important IMDb Rating. This is perhaps the most essential part of the IMDb Page. IMDb uses a "weighted" formula rather than an arithmetic one. A weighted average means that some votes have more weight than others. A film is rated on a scale of 1 to 10. With the score, IMDb indicates the number of users who voted. Though it is frustrating to many, IMDb will not disclose its methods. Doing so, they fear, may drive some sharpies to find ways to override the system. IMDb also takes precautions to prevent ballot stuffing. Only IMDb registered users can vote (from 1 to 10). Users can vote as many times as they want but every vote will replace the previous one. A rating will not be displayed unless the film receives a minimum of five votes.

The IMDbPro.com Feature. Whereas a listing on IMDb is free, subscribing to IMDbPro comes with a fee. Presently it's $19.99 per month or $149.99 per year. Being a subscriber entitles you to the following benefits:

• Listing your resume with photos.

• Adding demo reels online.

• Browsing casting notices and auditions.

• Posting casting notices and receiving submissions.

• Viewing credits, background, and contact information for major film and TV professionals.

• Viewing projects in development and pre-production, and the people involved in them.

• Receiving the daily "Industry News."

IMDb offers a one-month free trial subscription.

Making Your Film Available for Download. The video content on IMDb is in Adobe Flash format, the standard for video on the Internet. This is the same technology used by YouTube, Vimeo, LiveLeak, and practically all other video content providers. The Flash plugin is available for all major browsers and operating systems. Version 9.0 or higher of the Flash plugin is highly recommended for videos on IMDb.com. If your device does not support Flash, IMDb will attempt to play the video via HTML5.

Chapter 5
Financing—A Big Hurdle

> "Cinema should make you forget you are sitting in a theater."
>
> —Roman Polanski

You've maxed out your credit cards and borrowed every last cent from friends and relatives. You sold your car and took a second mortgage on your home. You still do not have enough money to finish and market your film. It's a hurdle you'll have to overcome. Otherwise, no film.

Crowdfunding is the option of choice for most filmmakers. Because it's such an important source of financing, the next chapter is totally devoted to this fairly new and important tool for raising money.

But crowdfunding has not totally replaced other tried and true methods for raising cash. You should also consider the following:

Grants. The key to success in getting a grant is to prepare a comprehensive, well-written, and well-organized submission package. Your film should also comply with the requirements set by the charity or foundation. Foundations generally consider the subject matter, geographic region, and the filmmaker's mission. Take a look at this excellent "How to Write a Grant Proposal" website, www.artistsnetwork.com/article/how-to-write-a-grant-proposal. For more tips on getting a grant for your film, see www.filmproposals.com/film-grant-tips.

Film Independent (www.filmindependent.org). Film Independent has teamed with the Alfred P. Sloan Foundation (www.sloan.org) to award filmmakers funds for producing films about scientists, engineers, and anything in the technology field. Every year at the Spirit Awards, Film Independent grants selected nominated films $25,000. Film Independent also awards "in-kind" grants allowing filmmakers to borrow, at no cost, production equipment.

Grant Space (www.grantspace.org). They are a division of the Foundation Center, a leading source of information about worldwide philanthropy. They list the following useful websites:

• Creative Capital (www.creative-capital.org). A national nonprofit organization that supports artists pursuing adventurous and imaginative work in film and video.

• GrantSelect (www.grantselect.com). A database of institutional and government grantmakers.

• Americans for the Arts (www.artsusa.org). An information clearinghouse that provides information on funding for individuals in all areas of the arts.

• Government Grants (www.grants.gov/indez.jsp). The official government site for information on federal grants and funding.

• Foundation Directory Online www.fconline.foundationcenter.org). They offer a comprehensive database of US grantmakers and their grants.

- United States Artists (www.unitedstatesartists.org/connect). Their stated mission is "to invest in America's finest artists and illuminate the value of artists to society." They were founded in 2005 with initial funding from The Ford Foundation, The Rockefeller Foundation, The Prudential Foundation, and The Rasmuson Foundation. Grants are awarded yearly to artists working in eight categories, one of which is film.

State Tax Credits. Most states offer tax credits and financial assistance to filmmakers selecting locations within the state. The usual requirements are as follows:

- Film must be approved.

- A minimum time must be spent filming in the state.

- Expenses allowed are usually defined. Acceptable expenses can be for equipment, construction of sets, meals, and lodgings.

- Preference is given if filming is in an economically undeveloped area and for hiring an in-state crew.

States offer credit three ways:

1. Straight Refund. When the film is completed, you'll receive a check for the amount allowed.

2. Transferable Credits. You can use the credits against your state income tax (if you reside in that state) or you can sell the credits to a broker (at a discount) or use them as collateral for a loan from an Asset Based Lender (ABL).

3. Non-Transferable Credits. You can only use the credits to reduce your state income tax and only if you are a resident of the state.

Every state has a Film Office, sometimes called a Film Commission. They should be contacted before you make the film to get the lowdown.

Finding a Sponsor. The local restaurant, florist, or food store might pay you something if you add their ad before the running of your film in a theater. Do not make it more than 30 seconds.

Product Placement. This should be planned before filming. Companies often pay if one of their products appears in the film. The product has to be clearly visible.

Chapter 6
Crowdfunding—A Viable Option

> "A style is not a matter of camera angles or fancy footwork; it's an expression, an accurate expression, of your particular opinion."
>
> —Karel Reisz

Crowdfunding is a popular way for filmmakers to raise money from a large number of people via the Internet. There are three parts to a crowdfunding campaign: (1) the filmmaker seeking the funds, (2) the donors, and (3) the organization (or platform) that handles the fundraising administration. The crowdfunding industry now raises over $5 billion worldwide.

There are two basic types of crowdfunding:

1. Rewards Crowdfunding. Filmmakers pre-sell the making of their films without incurring debt or sacrificing equity (shares). People donating money in this category are believers in the film or the filmmaker and are happy to be part of the experience. In return, they receive a reward (or gift), which could be a producing credit, a signed poster, a mug, or a free ticket to the opening. This is, by far, the preferred option for filmmakers.

2. Equity Crowdfunding. The investors receive shares in the film company. They become stockholders or partners, and have a financial stake in the outcome.

Most crowdfunding platforms work this way:

• There is no application fee, so there's no risk.

• You are responsible for setting up your marketing page, which should include videos and a trailer.

• You'll determine the dollar amount you want to raise and the length of the campaign, subject to company approval.

• You will have to specify the award or gift you will offer for each level of donation. For example, for a $50 donation, you can offer a mug or a signed poster. For a larger donation, you can offer a producer's credit.

• Most crowdfunding companies have a global reach, so you should consider this when designing your marketing page.

• Crowdfunding companies have different formulas for remitting the money raised. Know beforehand the company's policy.

• Anyone can participate as long as they comply with the company's guidelines.

• Funds received may be considered income by the IRS. Check with your accountant.

There are currently over two hundred websites with "crowdfunding" in their names. There is even an International Crowdfund Film Festival in Los Angeles every October. (www.crowdfundfilmsociety.com or info@icfff.org). The festival offers filmmakers an opportunity to connect with crowdfunding companies and consultants.

Here are four major crowdfunding platforms to consider:

Indiegogo (www.indiegogo.com). 15 million people from 224 countries visit this site each month. You receive the total amount of money raised, even if you do not reach your set goal. Of course, you will pay fees:

- 4% if you reach your goal

- 9% if you do not reach your goal

- 3%-5% per payment for payments made by credit card or PayPal

- $25 wire fee for overseas donations

- Additional currency exchange fees may apply

Kickstarter (www.kickstarter.com). This is an all-or-nothing deal. If you do not reach your goal, all the donations received will be returned and you will not be charged a fee. Since the start of the company in 2009, over $1 billion has been donated by more than 7 million donors. Their fees:

- 5% of the total raised

- 3% + $0.20 for each donation above $10.00

- 5% + $0.05 for each donation below $10.00

- You pay nothing if you do not reach your goal

• Additional fees may be charged for wire transfers, donations from overseas, credit card and PayPal payments, and currency exchanges

RocketHub (www.rockethub.com). This company offers access to the RocketHub's Crowdfunding Success School to assist filmmakers. You'll receive the total amount raised, even if you do not reach your goal. The company offers assistance in determining the goal. The television network A&E has partnered with RocketHub to form the A&E Project Startup. This can lead to funding of the film by A&E, on-air exposure, and a write-up in the A&E bi-annual magazine. Their fees:

• 4% if you reach your goal

• 8% if you do not reach your goal

• 4% commission fee

• 4% credit card fee

• Additional fees may be charged for wire transfers, donations from overseas, credit card and PayPal payments, and currency exchanges

Kapipal (www.kapipal.com). Kapipal is a European-based company specializing in reaching overseas donors. They can handle donations in foreign currencies and speak several languages. Payment by PayPal is required. Their fees:

• 4% of the total funds raised

• 2.9% + $0.30 for each donation coming from the US

• 3.9% + $0.30 for each donation coming from other countries

Some Tips for Achieving Success with Crowdfunding:

• Your initial donations will come from friends, relatives, and associates. Make sure they all see your site.

• You will be competing with hundreds of other filmmakers seeking donations. Use a graphics professional to design your site. Add exciting videos and an enticing trailer.

• You have to promote your campaign. The companies will not lift a finger. Work overtime marketing your campaign on the major social networks and search engines.

• Be grateful for any donation received. E-mail "thank you" notes. Donors will appreciate your graciousness and tell their friends to also donate. It can become viral.

• Make your pitch personal. Include your background and the reasons why you made the film, but stay away from controversial subjects like politics or religion.

• Don't stint on the rewards. Set up different levels offering more generous rewards for higher donations. Cheapskates will always have a hard time raising money.

• You might want to do an e-mail blast using a company like PRWeb (www.prweb.com). See Chapter 8.

• Insert a link to your film's website. And on your film's website, insert a link to your crowdfunding page.

The JOBS Act, which was signed into federal law in 2012 and recently approved by the SEC, offers interesting possibilities for crowdfunding. The JOBS Act allows filmmakers to raise up to $1 million from a large number of accredited investors by selling securities through a broker or SEC-approved funding portal. When sold through these qualified intermediaries, crowdfunded securities are exempt from certain regulations and state securities laws. See the Security and Exchange Commission's website, www.sec.gov, for more information.

Chapter 7
Hiring a Publicist—A Key Player

> "The more opinions you have, the less you see."
>
> —Wim Wenders

If you are self-distributing your film, you'll need a publicist. Case closed.

With the development of excellent low-cost cameras and post-production software, the market is now glutted with indie films all looking for that golden opportunity. That's a reality you'll have to address. You'll need to find that unique hook that will set your film apart from the herd. Getting favorable reviews is a great hook, especially from the major media in New York and Los Angeles. Everyone who matters in the film industry reads the reviews in the Friday *New York Times*, when most new films open. Not every film is reviewed by the major publications. So, to improve your chances, you'll need to hire a competent publicist. It's not something you can do well on your own.

As a filmmaker on a starvation budget, hiring a publicist can easily be your most expensive outlay. This need not be the case. Here are two way to keep the cost down:

1. Stay away from the larger PR firms with multiple departments and high-priced associates. You're not looking to land interviews on network talk shows or get write-ups in the entertainment

publications. An ideal firm would be a boutique with a few employees wearing multiple hats. Or, better yet, a independent publicist who works on his or her own.

2. Request the publicist to work in only three areas: (a) contact the major film critics and make sure they screen the film, (b) write and mail press releases, and (c) compile and distribute production notes. For an indie film, that's all you really want the publicist to do. And the cost should be considerably less than for a full-fledged PR campaign.

Filmmakers often ask me if they should allocate funds for advertising. Save the dough. The review is the best ad you could buy. A good review in *The New York Times* is worth a million bucks.

An easy way to save money is to prepare as much material as possible in advance. Publicists charge for their time. The more you do on your own, the less the publicist has to do.

You should provide the publicist with the following:

• High-res film stills (minimum 300 dpi). Use a professional photographer and have the photos taken while shooting the film. Each photo should in some way define the film. Avoid personal shots.

• A short synopsis (three or four lines).

• A long synopsis. Minimum half page.

• Job titles and bios of all key players and producers.

- Film background and a few lines about why you made the film.

- How the film was shot and something about the locations.

- Trivia about the making of the film.

- Minimum of 25 DVDs. Most film critics no longer attend theater screenings.

The job of hiring a publicist can indeed be daunting, especially to an indie filmmaker. Here are a few tips on how to find the right person:

- Get references. Ask to speak to other filmmakers the publicist handled. When calling references, ask the following: How many write-ups and reviews did the film receive? Did the publicist meet all your expectations? Was the publicist easily accessible? Did the publicist have any drawbacks? (If the answer is "no drawbacks," discard this reference. It's not an honest one.)

- Ask about the genres handled by the publicist. If your film is a documentary about climate change and the publicist has been handling mostly horror films, look for someone else.

- Make sure the publicist has seen the film and is genuinely enthusiastic. A publicist who is ready to sign the agreement before seeing the film is a publicist who should be shown the front door.

- Determine how accessible the publicist will be. You don't want one who only works Monday to Friday, nine to five. A good publicist, like a good pediatrician, never clocks out.

• Spend time schmoozing with the publicist. Your chemistry has to be good. Talk not only about the film but about the books you've read, films you've seen, vacations taken, and even the weather.

• Make sure the publicist understands the full meaning of the your film. Just liking the film is not enough.

• If you've seen a film you thought was well publicized, ask the distributor for the name of the publicist. It could be a good lead.

• Check the publicist's website. A badly designed website that's difficult to navigate is indicative of the work you can expect.

• The theater where your film will be playing may have an in-house publicist. Using the theater's publicist can save you money.

Here are some things NOT to discuss with your publicist because they will mark you as an amateur:

• Getting your film accepted by one of the hot film festivals.

• Getting a specific critic to review the film.

• Guaranteeing that your film will be reviewed by every publication.

• Guaranteeing that your film will surely be picked up by all the digital platforms and cable VOD stations.

• Picking the publicist's brain before you sign on.

• Asking for their media contacts.

- Asking for an estimate of the box office income.

Once you have selected the publicist, you'll want them to submit a formal agreement (which should be checked by an attorney). Make sure the agreement includes:

- The job the publicist will be doing which should be clearly and completely described.

- The budget for the campaign should be capped. Be sure to define expenses you will cover.

- The fees should be defined. Some publicists charge an hourly rate; some charge a monthly flat rate.

- Limit the duration of the project. An indie film should not need more than two months.

- Request that any expenditure above a certain amount requires your approval.

- Indicate the frequency of reports and actions taken. Agree on a weekly report, at minimum.

- Request a copy of every review and/or write-up the film receives.

I've admired the publicist and consultant Joan Stewart for many years. She gave some sage advice about PR etiquette in a recent article: "Stay humble. Trust a professional to do the job right. Communicate professionally. Document instructions with an e-mail or a letter. Express gratitude if you feel the job was well done. And, finally, do not burn bridges. Regardless of how a business relationship is severed, make a respectful exit. You never know when you will cross paths again or when a publicist might be able to pull a favor for you." Amen!

Chapter 8
DIY Press Releases—It's Easy

> "The enemy of art is the absence of limitations."
>
> —Orson Welles

Launching your film successfully requires that you hire a competent publicist. You'll need a publicist to contact the major film critics in order to get the film reviewed. The publicist will also write and mail press releases and compile and distribute production notes.

However, you can supplement the work of your publicist by writing and sending your own press releases (DIY) to the following outlets:

• Local newspapers that your publicist will probably not cover.

• Religious publications: church, synagogue, temple.

• Social organizations and clubs.

Here are some tips on writing your own press release:

• Write in the third person. Avoid "I" or "We" unless you are using it in a direct quote.

• Be brief. Maximum length should be 500 words. Do not exceed one page.

• Get to the point up front. You'll lose the reader if your first sentence is not relevant.

• Avoid making it sound like a sales pitch and do not use grandiose adjectives.

• Do not insert your opinions.

• Avoid film jargon, which may not be understood by people not in the business.

• Proofread and proofread again. A spelling or grammatical mistake will kill your message.

• Follow the standard press release format. The page should include: (1) the headline, (2) subhead elaborating the headline, (3) city and date of the release, (4) your contact information, and (5) a link to your film's website.

E-Blast PR Companies: There are companies that will blast your press release to thousands of outlets in their database. Most of these companies will critique your release and offer tips on writing the release. They also offer analytics so you can measure the effectiveness of your release. You'll know how many people read your release and the outlets that published it. An important benefit is that your release may help increase your discoverability on Google, Bing, and Yahoo.

Here are three E-Blast PR companies you may want to consider using:

PRWeb (www.service.prweb.com). They reach 250,000 subscribers and 30,000 journalists. The basic cost is $99.00 per release. You choose five industries and two regions you want to reach.

iReach by PR Newswire (www.ireach.prnewswire.com). Their focus is online and social media marketing. They blast to more than 1,600 websites and allow you to add photos and videos. They also offer social media sharing that will increase your opportunity for retweets, shares, and likes. You can share your news with a selection of the company's 48 industry-focused Twitter feeds and their thousands of followers. The basic cost is $129.00 per release.

Newswire LLC (www.newswire.com). Their focus is the online, print, and social media outlets. They allow you to include images, logos, and video embeds. They offer one introductory release for free. For $79.00 per month, you will be entitled to two press releases per month.

NOTE: All prices quoted are subject to change. I quoted the basic, introductory cost for each company. Upgrades are offered for an additional cost.

Chapter 9
Finding a Distributor—
Who Knows? You May Get Lucky!

"An audience can live without a movie, but a movie cannot live without an audience."

—Amit Kalantri

Finding a distributor has become harder than getting a toddler accepted to a New York City nursery school. Unless you have a track record or your film features a few well-known actors, your chances are below nil. If a distributor does pick up your film, it will probably be without an advance. And, lastly, if you do receive an advance, consider it the only money you'll ever see from the distributor.

This is enough to make you reach for extra-strength Prozac. And yet, who knows? You may hook up with a distributor and be given a nice advance.

Don't start celebrating until you check the following:

• How long has the distributor been in business? Be wary if it's under three years.

• What kind of films have they distributed? They should have handled your type of films. If you've made a documentary, you don't want a distributor that specializes in sci-fi films.

• Have the distributor list the theaters they plan to book in the key cities, especially New York and Los Angeles.

• What's the distributor's reputation with these theaters? Check by calling the managers of one or two of these theaters.

• How frequently will you receive reports? Should be weekly.

• How frequently will you receive payments? Payment should be made within 30 days after the end of the run.

• Check out the office staff. Do they have specialists handling every aspect of film distribution?

• What's the deal with ancillary rights? This includes DVD sales, digital and cable VOD sales, and foreign sales. Don't let the distributor strangle you by requiring long-term exclusivity. What will be your percentage of the income?

• Define the territories the distributor will handle.

• Review grosses, both theatrical and digital, of past films handled by the distributor.

• Have the right to reject any booking if the deal is not to your liking.

• Define expenses. Best to put a cap on them.

• Request the right to sell DVDs on your website and at theaters.

Having a professional, competent distributor can be a feather in your cap. It is also prestigious. But be aware that you'll incur expenses:

• You'll need an entertainment lawyer to review the agreement and protect your interests.

• You'll have to provide deliverables, which will be itemized in the agreement. This will include a trailer, posters, a hard drive or digital file, etc.

• You may need to purchase Errors and Omissions (E&O) insurance.

• The distributor might require you to attend openings at your own expense.

• You'll need to provide a Quality Control Report (QC) from an acceptable lab. Some digital platforms will do this for you.

• You'll have to spend money to clear all rights.

• The distributor will provide the publicist. But you'll have to provide the necessary documents and photos to compile the production notes and write the press release.

One important DON'T: Don't ask the distributor to predict the film's gross. Even the big studios find this difficult to do. Hope for the best. Hope the distributor never loses interest in your film, and hope, heaven forbid, that the distributor does not go bankrupt.

Chapter 10
National Distribution—Is It Still Worth Doing?

"Pain is temporary, film is forever."

—John Milius

By far, the most important U.S. cities in which to open your film are New York and Los Angeles. The film industry focuses on these two cities when evaluating films. They devour the reviews in *The New York Times* and the *Los Angeles Times*, and they feverishly analyze the grosses reported by the databasing company Rentrak.

You should consider opening your film in other cities, especially if your film did well in New York or Los Angeles. It will give your film added exposure and enhanced credibility. However, know that self-distributing your film around the country will not be without cost. Here's why:

• Theaters prefer to book films submitted by approved distributors. If they decide to book your film without a distributor, they may (not always) require that you hire a local publicist to ensure that the film critics review the film.

• Theaters will often want you to spend a minimum on advertising.

• Your only option may be to four-wall (rent the theater). You will incur the above expenses plus the cost for renting the theater. However, you will keep 100% of the box office income. If the theater books the film on a regular basis, you will receive a percentage of the box office, usually between 25% and 35%.

Large arthouse theaters (and arthouse chains) have bookers selecting the films to be played. These are the people you want to romance. Smaller mom-and-pop theaters will probably assign a staff member to do the booking.

Competent, experienced bookers select films they feel will provide the best return. They have to make some very tough decisions. A theater's screen is like an airline seat or a hotel room: once the day passes, anything unsold cannot be sold again. Bookers must guess right most of the time or they will be looking for another job.

Your film will thus have to fight for the attention of the booker. Having a persuasive website and an enticing trailer helps. Persistence is important. Follow up with phone calls and e-mails. And make sure to thank the bookers for their consideration. List the film's achievements: reviews, awards, festivals attended, endorsements, and so forth.

If the booker gives your film the thumbs-up, control your enthusiasm. Negotiate:

• Check the type of films the theater has played in the past. Will your film fit with that type of lineup?

• Request the grosses of the films that played the previous week.

• What auditorium will your film be assigned? Most theaters have multiple auditoriums. They vary in size and in decor.

• How long will the run be? Ask for one week, or, at minimum, a long weekend (Friday, Saturday, and Sunday).

• What are the chances of extending the run? What will the film have to gross for it to be extended?

• What will you earn? The standard is that you will receive between 25% and 35% of the box office income. With a four-wall, you'll receive 100% of the box office income. Sorry, folks. Concession income is off limits. That belongs to the management.

• Request box office numbers after each show. Most theaters are now computerized so this should not be a problem. Wave goodbye to the booker who says you'll have to wait until the end of the run for numbers.

• Know when you will get paid. Thirty days after the completion of the run is standard.

• Ask about using the theater's publicist.

• Ask about the theater's discounted ad rates.

A major mistake is wasting your time and money pursuing a theater highly unlikely to book your type of film. Indie films will rarely see the inside of one of the major multiplexes like AMC or Regal. Receiving too many rejections can be deadly to your self-esteem.

There are three types of theaters you should consider:

1. Arthouse chains. You can cover many cities with one phone call.

2. Independent arthouse theaters. They are more compassionate to the struggling filmmaker.

3. The non-profit theaters. They are not driven to make a profit (how nice that is), so they can take a chance with your film.

Here are the big **arthouse chains**:

LANDMARK THEATERS
2222 South Barrington Avenue
Los Angeles, CA 90064
www.landmarktheaters.com
888-724-6362

The largest theater chain in the US dedicated to exhibiting and marketing independent and foreign films. Locations and theaters: Atlanta (Midtown Art Cinema), Baltimore (Harbor East), Berkeley (Shattuck Cinemas), Boston (Embassy), Chicago (Century City), Dallas (Magnolia), Denver (Mayan), Detroit (Main Art Theater), Houston (River Oaks Theater), Indianapolis (Keystone Art Cinema & Glendale 12), Los Angeles (Westside Pavilion & Ritz V Landmark), Milwaukee (Oriental), Minneapolis (The Uptown), New Orleans (Canal Place Cinema), New York (Sunshine), Oakland (Piedmont), Palo Alto (Aquarius), Philadelphia (Ritz East &Ritz at the Bourse), San Diego (Hillcrest Cinemas), San Francisco (Embarcadero & the Kabuki), Seattle (Harvard East & the Neptune), St. Louis (Plaza Frontenac & the Tivoli), Washington, DC (Bethesda Row & East Street Theater).

PACIFIC THEATRES ENTERTAINMENT COMPANY
120 North Robertson Boulevard
3rd Floor
Los Angeles, CA 90048
www.pacifictheaters.com
310-657-8420

A chain showing more upscale independent film. Locations and theaters: Chatsworth, CA (Pacific Winnetka 21), Culver City, CA (Pacific Culver Stadium 12), Glendale, CA (Pacific Glendale 18), Glenview, IL (Pacific Glen Stadium 10), Lakewood, CA (Pacific Lakewood 16), Los Angeles, CA (Pacific Grove 14), Northridge, CA (Pacific Northridge Center 10), Sherman Oaks, CA (Pacific Sherman Oaks 5).

SUNDANCE CINEMAS
32998 Denver Springs Drive
Westlake Village, CA 91361
www.sundancecinemas.com
818-889-8562

Founded in 2007 and still owned by Robert Redford. Locations and theaters: Houston (Sundance Cinemas), Madison, WI (Sundance 608), San Francisco (Sundance Kabuki), Seattle (Sundance Cinema Seattle), West Hollywood (Sundance Cinema Sunset 5).

READING INTERNATIONAL, INC.
6100 Center Drive
Suite 900
Los Angeles, CA 90045
www.readingcinemasus.com
213-235-2240

A real estate development company with interests in movie theaters. Locations and theaters: LaMesa, CA (Grossmont Center 10), Manville, NJ (Manville 12), San Diego (Gaslamp 15, Town Square 14, & Carmel 12).

CITY CINEMAS
189 Second Avenue
New York, NY 10003
212-871-6833

A subsidiary company of Reading International, they operate the Angelika Film Centers in New York; Fairfax, VA; Washington, DC; Dallas, TX; and Plano, TX.

LAEMMLE THEATERS
11523 Santa Monica Boulevard
Los Angeles, CA 90025
www.laemmle.com
310-478-1041

Established in 1938 and owned and operated by Robert Laemmle and his son Greg Laemmle. Popular arthouses in the Los Angeles area. Locations and theaters: Beverly Hills (Music Hall 3), Claremont (Claremont 5), Encino (Town Center 5), Los Angeles (Royal), North Hollywood (Noho 7), Pasadena (Playhouse 7), Santa Monica (Monica 4).

ALAMO DRAFTHOUSE
13809 North Highway 183
Austin, TX 78750
512-219-7800

A new chain expanding rapidly through franchising. Theaters are mostly located in Texas but spreading to other cities: Phoenix, Los Angeles, Littleton, Baton Rouge, Kalamazoo, Kansas City, Omaha, Yonkers, Brooklyn.

Independent Theaters. Privately owned theaters that, hopefully, will be more sympathetic to fledgling filmmakers:

Lincoln Plaza Cinema
1886 Broadway
New York, NY 10023
www.lincolnplazacinema.com
212-757-0359

Cinema Village
22 East 12th Street
New York, NY 10003
www.cinemavillage.com
212-924-3363

Quad Cinema
34 West 13th Street
New York, NY 10011
www.quadcinema.com
212-255-2243

New Beverly Cinema
7165 West Beverly Boulevard
Los Angeles, CA 90036
www.newbevcinema.com
323-938-4038

Roxie Theater
3117 16th Street
San Francisco, CA 94103
www.roxie.com
415-863-1087

Music Box Theater
3733 North Southport Avenue
Chicago, IL 60613
www.musicboxtheatre.com
773-871-6604

Miami Beach Cinematheque
1130 Washington Avenue
Miami Beach, FL 33139
www.mbcinema.com
305-673-4567

Movies of Delray
7421 Atlantic Avenue
Delray, FL 33446
www.moviesofdelray.com
561-638-0020

The Nonprofit Theaters

Their mandate is to give preference to new filmmakers and to show films that may not have a shot at a commercial run. They are funded by foundations and private donors so they can take more risks than profit-making theaters and chains:

Film Forum
209 West Houston Street
New York, NY 10014
www.filmforum.org
212-727-8110

The Elinor Bunin Munroe Film Center
Film Society of Lincoln Center
165 West 65th Street
New York, NY 10023
www.filmlinc.com/about/the-elinor-bunin-munroe-film-center
212-875-5367

Gene Siskel Film Center
164 North State Street
Chicago, IL 60601
www.siskelfilmcenter.org
312-846-2600

Houston Cinema Arts Festival
4409 Montrose Boulevard
Suite 150
Houston, TX 77006
www.houstoncinemaartsfestival.org
713-429-0420

Jacob Burns Film Center
364 Manville Road
Pleasantville, NY 10570
www.burnsfilmcenter.org
914-773-7663

Cleveland Cinematheque
11141 East Boulevard
Cleveland, OH 44106
www.cia.edu/cinematheque
216-421-7450

Belcourt Theatre
2102 Belcourt Avenue
Nashville, TN 37212
www.belcourt.org
615-383-9140

Cinema Arts Centre
423 Park Avenue
Huntington, NY 11743
www.cinemaartscentre.org
631-423-3456

Circle Cinema
10 South Lewis Avenue
Tulsa, OK 74104
www.circlecinema.com
918-585-3504

Chapter 11
Foreign Sales—A Rich Market

"Eighty percent of success is showing up."

—Woody Allen

Without foreign sales, most Hollywood studios would be in big trouble today. Without foreign sales, some studios would have gone bankrupt. *50 Shades of Grey* opened with a $90 million weekend gross in North America. However, it grossed $150 million overseas. The sci-fi film *Battleship*, starring Liam Neeson and Rihanna, would have been a loser with a gross of only $65 million in North America, but the $237 million it grossed overseas made it a success. *Gulliver's Travels* grossed $42 million in North America and $150 million overseas. To date, *Birdman* has grossed $870 million in North America and a whopping $2.5 billion overseas. Recently, the Motion Picture Association of America (MPAA) predicted that 70 percent of total box office grosses will come from foreign markets. The big five overseas markets are China, Japan, India, Russia, and Western Europe.

Obviously, these differences in box office grosses would not apply to indie films and, especially, to documentaries. These kinds of films simply do not sell well overseas. However, a low-budget indie film does not have to gross millions to turn a profit. Good indie films will always find an audience in the major overseas markets. Some films will have more success overseas than others. Foreign filmgoers will have difficulty understanding many comedies, especially the ones with an American slant.

Documentaries are a hard sell because foreign viewers expect to see them for free on local TV. Mysteries, action, monster, and sci-fi films have a better shot of success overseas. Film consultant Wendy Bernfeld offers this insight: "Uniquely, American programs don't do very well in the international marketplace. World history, nature and wildlife, buried treasure stories, science, and technology stories all do well. American social issues or narrow political films are a much harder sell. The international marketplace looks for programs that are somehow universal."

The easiest, most economical, most productive way for filmmakers to reach overseas markets is to sign up with the major digital platforms. Amazon Instant Video is available in England, Japan, Germany, and Austria. iTunes is available in over 60 countries. Netflix is available in England, France, Austria, Switzerland, Belgium, Luxembourg, and Germany. And, happily, all of these companies are adding more countries each year. In a very short time, they will cover the entire world. Interestingly, these digital platforms have not become as popular overseas as they are in North America. But that will change. Trust me.

Another way to sell or book your film overseas is through your website. Remember, your website can be accessed all over the world. And you should list your film on the major free streaming platforms like VHX, Vimeo, and YouTube.

To implement the above, you should secure the services of an international sales agent. Booking films overseas is far too complex for most filmmakers to undertake on their own. Mark Litwak, a leading entertainment lawyer, said it best: "Most filmmakers have no clue how to go about licensing their films, for instance to a Turkish buyer, and what terms would be acceptable.

Moreover, they don't even know who the buyers are in most territories."

Here's why you need an international sales agent:

• They will represent you at the leading trade shows: Cannes, Berlin, AFM, Mip, and MipCom. Most have a booth and/or hospitality suite to pitch the films they represent (including yours).

• They set up screenings for potential buyers and bookers.

• They have relationships with the major players in the major markets.

• They know how to negotiate the best deal and the kind of licenses that will work for your film.

• They will distribute promotional material, film and video masters, trailers, screeners, and photos.

• They will monitor sales and collect and transmit to you any income generated.

• They will advise you as to the best markets for your film.

• They will transmit the deliverables to the buyers and bookers and collect them when the film ends its run.

How do you find the right international sales agent? You can Google listings, check the program guides of the major film festivals, and get referrals from other filmmakers.

Before signing up with an international sales agent, go through this checklist:

• Check their website. It will give you an idea of the kind of work to expect.

• How long have they been in business? Avoid someone with less than three years' experience.

• Get a listing of the recent films they represented. Did they succeed? Were they similar to your type of film?

• Favor sales agents that are smaller and more personal. You film may get lost in the hands of a big-time sales agent.

• Do not consider a sales agent who does not feel it's necessary to see your film before signing on.

• Avoid sales agents who do not fully understand your film or are not totally enthusiastic. Test them by asking them specific questions about the film.

• Request to see the sales agent's standard agreement. There may be sections in the agreement that will be unacceptable. Better to find out early in the game.

• Ask the agent to list the major countries handled. Have them give you a high/medium/low sales projection for each country or territory.

• Make sure the sales agents are as familiar with the TV markets as the theatrical markets. TV stations are currently the biggest buyers of US films.

• Before seeing the agreement, talk about the fee, the number of years of exclusivity, your cut of the income generated, the capping of expenses, the frequency of sales reports, when you will receive payments, and a possible advance. Absolutely, do not pay the sales agent anything up front. Anyone who asks for money up front is probably not legitimate.

• Define the sales agent's specialty. Some are experts in TV sales and some in theatrical sales. The good ones know both very well.

• Check out the people working in the sales agent's office.

Other important things to keep in mind:

• Make sure to make a 50-minute version of your film, which many TV stations require.

• The best place to meet and mingle with international sales agents is at the film festivals.

• Subtitles—you'll need them. However, before spending a dime, check to see if the buyer or booker will pay for it. Often, they do.

That all-important agreement. It can be a mind-boggling, multi-page, single-spaced nightmare. That's why you'll need an entertainment lawyer. Do not use a lawyer with a general practice or your brother-in-law who will not charge you much. The film business is highly specialized and prone to some clever hanky-panky. Only a competent entertainment lawyer will prevent you from getting ulcers. Having said all that, you should discuss with your attorney the following:

• The agent's percentage. The going rate is around 25% of the revenue generated. If it's much less, be wary. The sales agent may not exert maximum effort to promote your film.

• Term. Sales agents will want exclusivity for a set number of years. Most sales agents will know within two years if your film is going to fly. Therefore, try for a max of five years of exclusivity. If the agent requires more time, insert a clause that, if certain objectives are not reached at certain levels, you'll have the right to rescind the agreement.

• Expenses. Define what these expenses will be. Require that they be approved in advance. Request a cap. Creative accounting is very popular these days in the film business.

• Changes. Any changes in the film or in the editing should require your approval.

• Advertising and promotion. The sales agent should guarantee a set amount that will be spent to advertise and promote your film. Determine the kind of advertising and promotion. Ensure that the money will be spent for your film alone and not combined with the other films represented by the sales agent.

• Indemnity. You should be protected if the agent breaches parts of the agreement and creates legal problems with any entity.

• Insurance. An Errors and Omissions (E&O) insurance policy is usually required. In most cases, this will be your responsibility.

• Status reports. The sales agent should send you a weekly status report.

• Payment. Define when and how you will be paid.

• Inspection of books and records. Absolutely! Indicate that the examination can take place anytime.

• Approval of licenses and deals. Any license or deal the sales agent negotiates should be subject to your approval.

• Arbitration clause. Indicate that the arbitration be held in the US and be binding. It should follow the guidelines of the American Arbitration Association.

• Deliverables. Each buyer or booker of your film will require that you deliver a lot of stuff. Specify what that will be.

• Territory. Define the territory to be covered.

• Warranties. You will have to assure the sales agent that you have cleared all the rights and that there are no copyright violations. However, the warranty should be to your "best knowledge and belief" and not absolute.

Chapter 12
DVD Sales—Still Alive and Kicking

> "Having a really good understanding of history, literature, psychology, sciences—is very, very important to actually being able to make movies."
>
> —George Lucas

It's true! Hollywood studios are no longer depending on DVD sales to bail them out. But it's too early to pound the last nail in the DVD coffin. Although DVD sales at Netflix dropped 19% in 2014, they still grossed $1.02 billion. Furthermore, Netflix still maintains 39 distribution centers in North America, and 7 million subscribers paid Netflix to mail them DVDs in those all too familiar red envelopes.

DVD sales represent 10% or more of gross sales for some of the big Hollywood films. Of the $150 million grossed by the film *Divergent*, $27 million came from DVD sales. *Maleficent* grossed $241 million plus $29 million in DVD sales.

That's why you, the indie filmmaker, must include DVD sales as part of your overall marketing campaign.

DVDs are:

• Profitable. They can be made for a buck and sold for $15 or more.

- Transportable. It's a convenient way to see films when traveling or on vacation.

- Great for families. It's fun to show a film at family gatherings, especially if there are kids around. These classics continue to be bestsellers every year: *Mary Poppins*, *The Wizard of Oz*, *The Polar Express*, and *Willy Wonka and the Chocolate Factory*.

- Better quality than they used to be. A Blu-ray DVD projected on a large flat-screen TV is extraordinary.

- Collectible. There's no better way to maintain a library of the old classics.

- They make great coasters on your coffee table.

Three Major Ways to Sell DVDs:

1. On your website.

2. Through one of the digital platforms, especially Netflix and Amazon.

3. In theaters and at film festivals.

My preference is Amazon.

- It's prestigious. The entire world has heard of Amazon. It's a feather in your cap to tell people, "My film is available on Amazon."

- You need not maintain an inventory. Amazon fulfills orders on an as-needed basis. There's no waste.

• Amazon will process sales, collect payments, and remit your share of the income.

• They are a stable company. No fear of them going out of business.

• No up-front fee.

• You keep all the rights.

• Amazon is not selective. It will accept most films.

• They will assign a UPC for free if you do not already own one.

• Amazon can easily convert your DVD into a high-quality video download and make it available on Amazon Instant Video.

Submitting Your Film to Amazon

• Submit your film to Create Space, the division of Amazon handling this program (www.createspace.com).

• You must adhere to Amazon's content guidelines and member agreement.

• Submit as a single ISO file.

• The content must be unencrypted.

• Your source must contain only AUDIO_TS and VIDEO_TS folders in the root directory of the disc.

- Amazon will not support inclusion of data or executable files on the DVD.

- Amazon recommends using Dolby Digital (AC-3) audio. However, PCM and DTS audio are also supported.

- Amazon accepts discs up to 4.6 GB in size.

- Only single-track DVDs are supported at this time.

Artwork. Amazon offers a service called "Cover Creator" to design your DVD's full wrap and disc face artwork. "Cover Creator" is an easy way to create eye-catching, professional-looking artwork—at no charge. Images may be in either JPEG or GIF (not animated or transparent) formats. RGB images are required. The resolution of all images must be 300 DPI. You may not use the standard DVD-Video logo on your materials. However, you may use the DVD logo included on the Amazon templates.

Your full-wrap image is a single artwork file that includes the front cover, spine, and back cover. Here are the specs:

- Full-wrap cover image: 3300 x 2250 full bleed (image size, pixels), maximum 6 MB file size

- Disc face image: 1417 x 1417 full bleed (image size, pixels), maximum 2 MB file size

A small barcode will be added to the bottom of your disc artwork. This barcode is required for quality control purposes.

What you earn. Amazon's share is calculated by taking a percentage (usually 15%) of the list price, plus a fixed charge of

$4.95 per unit. If you sell a DVD for $25.00, you will earn $16.30. The breakdown is as follows:

List Price: $25.00
Less: ($4.95)
Less 15%: ($3.75)

Your income: $16.30

Sales tax (when applicable) and shipping charges are not included.

Amazon's cut may appear high, knowing that you can make DVDs for around $1 a unit. But you are being allowed to use the Amazon name and their administrative services. Also, most DVD manufacturers will require that you place a minimum order. This can be very costly if you are unable to sell the entire lot. Amazon has no minimum requirement.

Chapter 13
Cable Video On Demand—Better Days Are Coming

> "I didn't learn how to make a movie in film school. What I learned in film school was to express yourself with pictures and sound."
>
> —Martin Scorsese

The cable TV networks are stunned by the drop in viewers in recent years. In 2015, viewing of films on cable is down by 12%. The trade association, Cabletelevision Advertising Bureau, indicated that the primary reason for the drop is that "consumers are spending more time watching subscription streaming services like Netflix, Amazon Prime, and Hulu Plus."

This is very good news for indie filmmakers.

From the beginning, the cable networks focused on booking the Hollywood blockbusters, almost totally ignoring indie, foreign, and documentary films. This will change. Eventually, these networks will come to the realization that they need indie films to attract new subscribers and to retain their current subscribers.

The goal of indie filmmakers is to get their films listed on VOD (Video On Demand). The major cable channels have an On Demand feature. Viewers can scroll through an alphabetical list of films and pay to watch a film with a simple click. Film critic Anthony Kaufman facetiously commented that "since the films are listed alphabetically, if you're looking for an edge, it can't hurt to come up with a title for your movie that begins with the letter "A" or "B."

Here are the top 10 cable channels and the number of subscribers for each:

1. Comcast (22,376,000)

2. Time Warner Cable (11,030,000)

3. ATT U-verse (6,067,000)

4. Verizon FiOS (5,533,000)

5. Cox Communications (4,300,000)

6. Charter Communications (4,296,000)

7. Cablevision (2,715,000)

8. Bright House Networks (2,013,145)

9. Suddenlink Communications (1,171,000)

10. Mediacom (900,000)

As the cable companies start looking to include indie product, you can help your cause in the following ways:

• Have a strong theatrical opening in New York and/or Los Angeles.

• After the New York and/or Los Angeles runs, book at least 10 other major cities in the US

• Have your publicist provide you with a listing of the best reviews and any write-ups.

• Submit a well-written and organized package. If necessary, use a professional.

Many people in the industry criticize cable stations for their unwillingness to report grosses. Nolan Gallagher, head of Gravitas Releasing, defended the cable stations: "It's not that people are necessarily hiding things. The fact is that it's very complex. When an independent film opens in four theaters in New York and Los Angeles, and those theaters report $10,000 for each box office, that's a very easy amount of information to compile and publicize. But with VOD, we're talking about over 100 different operators, each with its own way of compiling and disseminating information."

In a recent article in *The New York Times*, "Viewers Start to Embrace Television on Demand," writers Brian Stelter and Amy Chozik wrote that "some providers, Comcast among them, see VOD as a savior—a way to make programming more accessible and retain cable subscribers."

Here are ways cable companies will be great for indie filmmakers:

• They are hooked up to millions of homes across the country.

• On Demand is easy to navigate. It does not require a password, a username, or additional billing.

• Films can be viewed right on the TV without the need of a special device.

• Viewers can see films anytime they want.

• If your film is picked up, chances are it can remain "live" for a long period of time.

Submitting Your Film. After you compile your package (see above), you'll have to submit your film through a well-connected distributor. You can't submit it directly to the cable station. Acceptance is not guaranteed, so be wary of distributors who promise you too much.

Here are three distributors with good connections you might try:

GRAVITAS VENTURES
209 Richmond Street
El Segunda, CA 90245
310-388-9353
info@gravitasventures.com

CEO Nolan Gallagher had years of experience working with Comcast and Warner Bros.

CINETIC MEDIA/FILM BUFFS
555 West 25th Street
4th Floor
New York, NY 10001
212-204-7979
info@cineticmedia.com

Founder John Sloss, a highly regarded entertainment lawyer, is also well-connected with the cable media.

CINEDIGM
1901 Avenue of the Stars
12th Floor
Los Angeles, CA 90067
424-281-5400
mkashden@cinedigm.com

CEO Chris McGurk had senior jobs at MGM, Universal Pictures, and the Walt Disney Studios.

Chapter 14
Four-Walling—Don't Dismiss It

> "In drama, the characters should determine the story. In melodrama, the story determines the characters."
>
> —Sidney Lumet

Simply defined, four-walling is renting a theater for a specific number of days for a specific price. During the four-walling period, you "own" the theater. You set the schedule. You will keep 100% of the box office income.

It's an option worth considering if you (1) prefer not to hook up with a distributor, (2) can't book a theater on a more traditional basis, (3) need a one-week run to qualify your film for an Oscar, and (4) want your film reviewed.

Many filmmakers think of four-walling as a sign of failure. This is often not the case. Many films have achieved success by four-walling. The other option is to do nothing and let the film die.

Four-walling a theater goes back a long way. In a recent article, film writer Scott Beggs wrote that it probably started as far back as 1919 when Oscar Micheaux rented space for his movie, *The Outsider*. It was so incredibly successful he eventually churned out 44 feature films in 29 years, most of them four-walled.

In the 1960s, American National Enterprises (ANE) four-walled a nature documentary *Alaska Safari* that attracted 5.5 million patrons over a five-year period. Several execs broke away from ANE to form SUNN Classic Pictures. They four-walled *Chariots of the Gods* (1974), *The Life and Times of Grizzly Adams* (1976), and *The Lincoln Conspiracy* (1976). All three films had successful runs.

Four-walling your film requires a negotiation between you and the theater manager. Good managers will want to screen the film first. They know that their patrons will be unaware that the film is a four-wall, so they must protect the reputation of the theater. Often a manager will reject your film even though you are willing to pay a rental fee. On the other hand, if the manager likes your film, you can probably cut a better deal.

Your negotiation should cover these points:

• Length of run. In New York and Los Angeles, the two key theatrical cities, film critics will rarely review a film that runs less than a full week. Some filmmakers, on a tight budget, opt to book their films for the weekend. That could be a mistake. Without a review, you are wasting your money four-walling.

• Price. Your bargaining position will depend on the manager's opinion of your film. Also, find out the theater's grosses from the previous week. Was it a slow week? This will be a factor in establishing the appropriate four-wall price. Also keep in mind that this is guaranteed income for the theater, unlike the other films on its schedule.

• Number of seats. Theaters with more than one auditorium can offer you a choice. Obviously, smaller theaters should cost less.

• Projectionist and projector. Are they included in the price?

• Publicist. In most cases this is not included. You'll need one to contact the film critics, write and mail press releases, and compile and distribute production notes. You can probably make a better deal using the theater's publicist.

• Box office income. It's pretty standard. You should receive 100% of the box office income. You are not entitled to any concession income. Bummer!

• DVD sales. You should have the right to sell DVDs of your film in the lobby (space permitting). Be prepared to give the theater a percentage of what you sell.

• Payment. It's important to define when you'll get paid. It's usually 30 days after the close of the run.

• Press screenings. Most film critics prefer to screen films at home or in their office. Some may prefer to screen your film in the theater. Negotiate a price with the theater manager for a morning screening. Any screening that will require canceling a regular show will be expensive.

• Extending the run. If the film does well, some theaters will extend the run on a regular basis, which means you will not have to four-wall and instead will receive a percentage of the gross.

• Advertising. Your film should be included if the theater runs an ad listing the films playing that week. Your film should also be listed in the movie indexes in the local newspapers and magazines.

• Promoting the film. It's your responsibility to promote your film. Distribute flyers throughout the neighborhood and work overtime promoting your film on the search engines and social networks.

• After the run. Make sure to collect your disc or hard drive as well as the posters and remaining flyers.

Final word: Do not four-wall beyond New York and Los Angeles. If your film gets good reviews and box office, you should be able to book your film in other cities on a regular basis.

Chapter 15
Streaming—It's the Future

> "Success or failure, there should always be a drive to keep on creating."
>
> —Henry Johnson, Jr.

In the corridors and the boardrooms in every Hollywood studio, the message is reverberating loud and clear—streaming films is the future. Research by the Digital Entertainment Group (DEG) found that for the first time, Americans spent more money streaming films than watching DVDs last year. In 2014, the combined sales for DVDs and Blu-ray discs hit $6.93 million. Streaming and video-on-demand sales grossed $7.53 million. The DEG Report concluded that "Consumers embraced the convenience and accessibility of purchasing and collecting digital content while studios reaped higher margins from these digital sales."

By 2017, Oscar voters will no longer be screening film nominees in theaters or on DVDs. Every qualifying film will be streamed to the voters. According to film journalist Tim Gray, "It can cost up to $800,000 and take three to six weeks to manufacture, watermark, and ship discs. In contrast, it only takes a few days to two weeks to encode and upload a title, at a fraction of the cost."

Indie filmmakers must consider streaming as a source of income for the following reasons:

• It's a way of renting or selling your film globally. Apple iTunes reaches over 60 countries; Amazon Instant Video can be accessed in England, Japan, Germany, and Austria; Netflix is available in England, France, Austria, Switzerland, Belgium, Luxembourg, and Germany. And, you can be sure, these companies will be adding more and more countries each year.

• Unlike a theatrical run, once a film is listed on one of these platforms, it can remain for a long time. Who knows—it may become an annuity.

Currently, there are over 200 companies streaming films to the general public. Choosing the right one can be mind-boggling, costly, and time-consuming. Most streaming outlets, despite their optimistic sales pitches, will not generate meaningful sales for your film.

Here are the big five outlets to consider:

Netflix. The leader in subscription streaming. With over 60 million subscribers and over 20,000 films available for streaming, it's the big kid on the block. But Netflix is the toughest when it comes to acquiring indie films, preferring the big Hollywood blockbusters and its own original content. When they select a film, they list it in their database. They then calculate how many people requested the film, called "Queue Demand." If the number is high, the film will be offered to subscribers. Netflix pays the filmmaker a fee for the right to stream the film an unlimited number of times for a set number of years. The good part of the deal is that you are, in effect, getting your dough up front. Netflix requires that you submit your film through an aggregator (distributor).

Apple iTunes. This is a transactional platform, which means customers pay for each film viewed. There is no requirement to subscribe. iTunes is selective and prefers to work with one of their approved aggregators. They list these approved aggregators on their website. Many distributors profess to have an "in" with iTunes. Chances are they will be submitting your film through one of the Apple-approved aggregators. iTunes pays filmmakers 70% of the income generated.

Hulu. It's a popular outlet because streaming films is free. Hulu makes its money selling the advertising that precedes the film. Again, you'll need to go though an aggregator. Hulu pays the filmmaker 50% of advertising income.

Amazon Instant Video. This company is not selective and will accept films directly from the filmmaker. Amazon pays the filmmaker 50% of the income generated. More on Amazon below.

Google Play. Like Amazon, Google Play is not selective and will accept films directly from the filmmaker. They also pay filmmakers 50% of the income generated.

Some other things to consider:

Closed Captioning. All films submitted to the streaming outlets must have closed captioning. That's the law. The cost varies from as low as $1 a minute to as high as $5 a minute. Use yellow type so the words can be more easily read, especially against a white background.

The Aggregator's Cut. The percentages paid by the streaming outlets (listed above) are BEFORE the cut the aggregators take. The average is 25%. However, keep in mind that the aggregator does do work on your film that includes encoding, checking the quality, and submitting the complete package.

Back to Amazon. Through their division Create Space (www.createspace.com), Amazon encourages filmmakers to book their films directly. It's not only free, but you'll avoid paying the aggregator's cut. Therefore, every filmmaker should list their film with Amazon, and the sooner, the better.

Here are Amazon's basic requirements:

• Do not submit videos with watermarks, color bars, or URLs.

• Ensure you have cleared all the rights.

• Closed captioning is required.

• Content must be on an authorized DVD provided as a single ISO file.

• ISO files must be unencrypted.

• Your source copy must be authored with a single Video Title Set (VTS), and you must place the main feature in one VTS under VTS_01. Discs authored with multiple VTS files cannot be accepted.

• Your source copy must contain only AUDIO_TS and VIDEO_TS folders in the root directory of the disc.

• Amazon does not support inclusion of data or executable files on DVD.

• In order to maximize playback compatibility, Amazon recommends a maximum total bit rate for the combined video and audio tracks of 6.5 Mbp/s (megabits per second).

• Amazon recommends using Dolby Digital (AC-3) audio. However, PCM and DTS audio are also supported.

• Discs up to 4.6 GB in size are acceptable.

• Only single-track DVDs are supported at this time.

Subtitles. Before you go through the expense of subtitling your film for a particular foreign market, find out if the local sales agent or distributor will do the job for you. Sometimes, they will.

The Last Word. In my opinion, the fee you pay an aggregator is well worth it. Many of the selective streaming outlets require it. The requirements of these outlets are so stringent and demanding that only an experienced company with a competent lab can navigate the process. This will also mean fewer delays in getting your film "live."

Here are but a few of the jobs performed by the aggregator:

• Ingesting and encoding your content from tape to file.

• Providing Quality Control (QC) for your film.

• Fixing minor macroblocking and interlacing audio drops and pops.

• Preparing metadata and poster art.

- Providing generic chaptering, if applicable.

- Offering a dashboard to view, order, and manage sales.

- Collecting the money and transmitting it to you on a timely basis.

Chapter 16
Facebook—One Billion Users and Counting

"Filmmaking is a miracle of collaboration."

—James McAvoy

It's simply incredible. Facebook now has over one billion users worldwide. There are 30 million active small business pages. Over 800 million users reach Facebook on their mobile phones. More than one half of the users visit Facebook every day. With such an enormous reach, you should consider advertising your film on Facebook. However, consider it only if you have something to sell (DVDs), or you are streaming your film from one of the digital platforms. Since Facebook is reaching people around the world, this becomes an easy way for them to rent or purchase your film.

Facebook is a great option for advertising indie films. Here's why:

• Setting up a business page is easy and it's free.

• You'll pay on a per-click or per-impression basis. You'll decide how much you want to pay per click (PPC) or per impression (people "looking" at your page), and on your monthly budget.

• You can define the market you want to reach in many different categories, such as age, gender, marital status, earnings, geography, and much more. Your ads will thus be reaching only the people you feel might be interested in seeing your film. It's very efficient.

• You can update, share opinions, and post new information on your page anytime you want.

• Your postings will generate comments and may spread like a virus.

• Facebook has a very informative analytic service that can tell you about the people who viewed your page.

• Most online advertising reaches only 38% of its intended audience. Facebook's average is 89%.

Starting out: Your first steps should be the following:

• Have your film's website sell DVDs.

• Check www.facebookforbusiness.com to get the lowdown.

• Make sure your film is available on a few of the major streaming and DVD platforms.

• Create a business page for your film.

Here are the steps to take for creating a business page:

• Go to www.facebook.com/pages/create.

• Click a page category.

• Select a more specific category from the drop-down menu and fill out the required information.

• Click "get started" and follow the on-screen instructions.

Facebook requires that the page name accurately reflects the subject of the page. It's best to select the name of your film for your page name. Easy. Facebook will not allow phrases that may be abusive or violate someone's rights, improper capitalization, the use of all capital letters except for acronyms, symbols or unnecessary punctuation, long descriptions or slogans, and misleading words or statements.

Creating the ad. Your goal is to motivate the viewer to click your ad and to look at the film's website. The website will be about your film and, more importantly, will tell the viewer how and where to purchase DVDs or stream the film. Facebook can help you create the ad and set it up. The ad cannot exceed 25 characters for the title and 135 characters for the body. The "Facebook Ads Guide" gives detailed information like specs for photos, available fonts, and a preview of the ad before it's published.

Some tips:

• Facebook is a social network. Don't ruffle feathers by selling aggressively or over-promoting yourself. Be friendly, outgoing, and chatty. Post some funny anecdotes about the film and perhaps a few tidbits about the cast or the crew. Be authentic. Be transparent.

• Keep updating your page. Talk about late news about your film, some recent experiences, some interesting stories.

• Engage with your fans. Respond to their comments.

• Use "We" instead of "I."

• Promote you Facebook Page wherever you can: on your website, film flyers and posters, even on your letterhead.

• Visit "Page Insights" regularly to learn about new Facebook applications.

• If necessary, have a professional design your page. Don't make it look cheap.

• Terms and conditions. Access "Facebook Statement of Rights and Responsibilities" for a complete listing. Facebook monitors your actions and will quickly and brutally pull the plug if you violate any of their rules.

Here are a few **Don'ts**:

• Post unauthorized commercial communications.

• Engage in unlawful multilevel marketing or pyramid schemes.

• Bully, intimidate, or harass any user.

• Provide false personal information.

• Share your password or let anyone else access your account.

• Promote get-rich schemes, firearms, prescription drugs, or adult paraphernalia.

• Violate any state or federal laws, regulations, and guidelines.

Chapter 17
Google AdWords—The #1 Search Engine

> "A lot of times you get credit for stuff in your movie you didn't intend to be there. "
>
> —Spike Lee

Filmmakers often ask me about where and how to advertise their films. And, of course, how much they should spend. I usually discourage spending anything on opening day, as I feel the review is the best ad you can buy, and it's free. If, heaven forbid, the review is not favorable, any ad you buy will not help the film. It would be money wasted.

The one exception is Google AdWords. This is perhaps the most economical, the most efficient, and the most effective form of advertising today. It's why so many newspapers and magazines are fighting to stay alive.

However, consider Google AdWords only if:

• The film is either a documentary or a feature about a specific issue. More on this later.

• You have a website selling DVDs of your film.

• You film can be streamed on one of the major platforms.

Google is the leading search engine in the world today. Millions access Google to get information about a product or a service. Google has replaced the Yellow Pages.

Your goal: It's simple. You want people to view your website, buy DVDs of your film, or stream your film from a digital platform. Since Google reaches a global market, you'll be able to attract customers from around the world.

Why only documentaries or features about a specific issue? People access Google to obtain information about a product or service. A documentary is basically a film about a specific subject. For example, a few years ago the very successful documentary *Bill W* opened, which was about William Griffith Wilson, the founder of Alcoholics Anonymous (AA). Many people interested in knowing more about alcohol abuse and remedies Googled this subject for information. After clicking these keywords, the viewer saw a listing of the many different sources on this subject. Many people were motivated to click the ad for *Bill W*. What they next saw was the website for the film.

Choosing "keywords" (sometimes called "search terms"). Your goal is to have your ad appear every time a person is searching for information that relates to the subject of your film. If you were the filmmaker for *Bill W*, you'd want your ad to appear every time a person searched keywords such as "Films about Alcoholism," "History of AA," "William Griffith Wilson," etc. When your ad is clicked, your website should appear on the screen.

Writing the ad. Google requires that the ad be a maximum of four lines:

The Headline. Maximum 25 characters.

The Body. Maximum two lines. Each line should not be more than 35 characters (70 characters total).

Your URL.

Setting the budget. With Google AdWords, you only pay if someone clicks your ad (called pay-per-click advertising). You decide the amount you want to pay per click and your maximum monthly budget. For example, you can specify that you will pay $5 per click, and you do not want to spend more than $100 per month.

Opening a Google AdWords account. Easy to do on their website, www.googleadwords.com. They also have a 24/7 help line, 1-800-877-2981. Opening an account is free.

Google Database. Make sure your film's website is included. You may need a professional to do this job.

An important note: Unlike conventional print or online advertising, there are no guarantees that your ad will appear. Much will depend on how many other ads were submitted for a specific keyword, the relevancy of your film, and your budget. If two or more ads are competing for space on the Google page, chances are that the ad with the higher budget will get preference. It takes some testing to determine the minimum you must spend to ensure that your ad will be listed, preferably on the first page. Each keyword may have several pages of listings. Getting your ad on the first page is vital.

Why Google AdWords is so effective:

- You only pay per click and you can set the budget.

- You can cancel anytime.

- You can change or tweak your ads to measure which ones work best.

- You will reach people interested in your film's subject.

- Google AdWords can be accessed on desktop computers, laptops, tablets, and most mobile devices.

- Google provides analytics to show how your ad is doing and how it can be improved.

- Google offers three months of consultancy for free.

Organic listings. In addition to paid advertising, Google includes many other listings that it deems relevant to the subject being searched. These are called organic listings. Having an organic listing is the closest thing to being in heaven because it's free and it will generate the most clicks. A recent survey indicated that organic listings will receive 80% more clicks than the ads. But don't fret. With millions of people searching for information, even getting a smaller percentage of clicks will make you a very happy camper. If your film is lucky enough to get an organic listing, cancel the ad.

Using a professional. There are plenty of charlatans out there who will guarantee, for a hefty fee, that they can get your film organically listed or ensure that your ad will appear on the first page. They will profess to know how to deal with Google's complex algorithms. Be wary. Google's methods are designed so that very few people can comprehend them. However, you may need a professional to ensure that your website has been included in Google's database, in composing the ad, in setting the budget, and monitoring the results. Most professionals either work on an hourly basis or on a monthly retainer.

How to make Google like you. The more "likable" you are to Google, the better chance you have of getting an organic listing and/or having your ad listed on the first page (preferably near the top). Here are some tips:

• Have a well-written, grammatically correct website. Google hates bad English, misspellings, and a website that's hard to navigate.

• Your ad should tie in with your website. The headline should define the subject of your film. A good ad is relevant.

• Use "www" in your domain name.

• Avoid listing numbers, exclamation points, and overused pitches like "Buy Now!" or "Great Bargain!"

• Ampersands save time and result in more clicks. Instead of using the word "and" use "&."

• Do not include prices. Your website will take care of this.

• Don't promise what you can't deliver. That applies to both the ad and the website.

• Be transparent and above board. Any hint of deviousness will kill you. Don't ask me how, but Google can sense this.

A final word. Do not become obsessed with the number of clicks. Since you are paying per click, you do not want to waste money having people unlikely to buy or stream your film click your ad. You can control this by limiting the keywords to the ones you feel will attract the people you want. For example, going back to the film, *Bill W*, keywords like "Remedies for Alcoholism" or "Alcohol Addiction" should attract the kind of people you want. A keyword like "Best Bars in New York" may generate plenty of clicks, but few of them will be people interested in seeing your film.

Chapter 18
LinkedIn—More Than a Job-Hunting Site

> "When given an opportunity, deliver excellence and never quit."
>
> —Robert Rodriguez

LinkedIn, to many, is simply the place to post a resume, a photo, a profile, and, hopefully, find a job.

LinkedIn also offers an excellent opportunity to advertise your film. It will allow you to reach only audiences that might be interested in seeing your film and it will motivate these people to view your website.

Like Facebook and Google AdWords, you control your costs with the "pay-per-click" model (PPC) or the number of people who view your page. LinkedIn is the world's largest professional network, with over 300 million members in over 200 countries.

The LinkedIn Ads Program. You specify the type of members you want to view your ad by selecting a target audience by job title, job function, industry, geography, age, gender, company name, company size, or LinkedIn group.

 You should only advertise on LinkedIn if:

- Your film is a documentary or deals with a specific issue.

- You are selling DVDs of your film on your website or digital platforms.

- Your film can be streamed from a digital platform.

Offering a documentary or a feature film on a special issue or topic is essential as members will be clicking your ad (and viewing your website) to obtain information about what your film is about. If your film is about "Hiking the Appalachian Trail," you'll want to attract only people who might be interested in this activity.

Getting started. It's easy. Create the ad, select the target audience, and set your budget. You determine how much you want to spend per click or each time a member views your ad (impression). You also determine the maximum amount you want to spend per day. Your ad will be reviewed by the customer support team. If it meets the LinkedIn ad guidelines, your ad will run within 24 hours.

Ad Specifics:

Headline. Maximum 25 characters.
Body. Maximum two lines, 35 characters each line.
Image/Photo. Placed on the left side of the ad (50 x 50 pixel image).
URL

Your ad may appear in various positions on any or all of the following pages:

Profile Page (when members view the profile of other members).
Home Page (the page users see when they log in to LinkedIn).
Inbox (the page users access for messages or for connecting).

Search Results Page (the page users see when searching for members by name).
Groups (groups specified to see your ad).

Cost. These are the basic costs. You can change the amounts whenever you wish. There are no contracts. You can cancel anytime. There is a $5 activation fee when you start.

1. Pay-Per-Click (PPC). Minimum is $2.00 per click.

2. Pay-Per-1,000 Impressions (CPM). You pay a set cost for each 1,000 times your ad is seen, no matter how many clicks you receive. Minimum is $2.00 per impression.

3. Minimum daily budget is $10.00.

Helpful ad tips:

• Choose words that grab the attention of your target audience.

• Motivate the viewers by offering something special, like a discount.

• Include awards or achievements like "Festival Winner" or "Oscar-Nominated Film."

• Include an image with the ad, like a poster.

• Review the LinkedIn advertising guidelines.

Maximizing results:

If you want to increase your click-through-rate (CTR) and/or increase the number of impressions, LinkedIn suggests the following:

• Try different types of ads and measure the ones that work best.

• Narrow your target audience so that your ad becomes more relevant.

• Break up each campaign into three or more sub-campaigns and write a different ad for each one.

• Make sure the ad is designed to promote your film.

Chapter 19
Trailers—Your Film's Resume

"Man is a genius when he is dreaming"

—Akira Kurosawa

A good trailer is almost as important as making a good film. And, as film consultant Jennifer Merin said, "A trailer that's carefully and beautifully edited will show the film's best attributes. It's just as challenging to edit a trailer as it is to edit an entire film, and sometimes harder. The trailer must be logical, constant, and an understandable introduction to the main characters, their circumstances, and to the tone of the film. The trailer must also establish that the filmmaker is competent and trustworthy."

Unless you are a super filmmaker, you should hire a professional to make your trailer. It's a huge factor in the success of your film. Making an effective trailer involves weaving together a diverse number of scenes, totally out of context, and with enough punch to motivate the viewer to see your film. A good trailer also includes appropriate music, striking graphics, and pleasant voiceovers. Here are factors to remember when producing your trailer:

• It's a vital part of your film's website. Viewers reading about your film will often click to see the trailer. If the trailer is compelling, they will be more apt to buy or stream the film.

• It can help attract investors.

• It's essential when promoting your film at festivals and film markets.

• It will help sell DVDs of your film to the retail chains, schools, colleges, and libraries.

• It's an essential part of your submission package to the digital platforms and cable VOD stations.

• It will help you pre-sell your film overseas.

• It will run in theaters before the film opens and generate interest in seeing your film.

Although you will probably be using a professional to produce the trailer, you should be hands-on and supervise the process. Here are some useful tips:

• Start work on the trailer after you finish the film, not before.

• Keep it under 2 1/2 minutes.

• Do not give away too much of the plot, and, most importantly, do not give away the ending.

• Use a professional to do the voiceovers.

• The trailer should inform the viewer as to the type of film it is. It should not mislead.

• The trailer should be geared to the type of audience you want to attract.

- Use top equipment. This is not the time to stint.

- Don't forget to include the title of the film, and, if prominent, the names of the actors.

- When running the trailer in a theater, indicate when the film will be opening.

- Make sure the trailer can be seen on mobile units, tablets, and the digital devices.

- End the trailer with a punchy line or a noteworthy quote.

- Screen the trailer as often as you can and encourage non-biased opinions.

- Be careful about inserting jokes. A lousy joke is a turnoff.

- Include dialogue. You do not want the trailer to sound like a music video.

- Mention past awards, quotes from good reviews, and appearances in film festivals.

Keep in mind that a person viewing your trailer will come to one of three conclusions:

1. I've got to see this film.

2. The film is a dog.

3. I have no idea what this film is about.

You want everyone to reach conclusion #1.

There is now a Golden Trailer Awards event held in New York every September. Judges are selected from top-level directors, producers, actors, writers, studio executives, exhibitors, advertising execs, and critics. The winner in 2014 was the trailer for *Gravity*.

Chapter 20
Film Festivals—Are They Worth the Cost?

> "The end of a picture is always an end of a life."
>
> —Sam Peckinpah

Are film festivals worth the cost? To answer that question, you must understand the following:

• With few exceptions, distributors are not paying any advances for films unless the filmmaker has a track record and the film has a few big-name actors.

• Filmmakers fortunate enough to get a distributor will receive minimal, if any, money in advance.

• Fewer distributors and important film executives are attending festivals.

• Attending film festivals is getting more expensive due to cutbacks in festival budgets. You'll most likely have to pay for transportation, hotels, food, and buying drinks for the distributors you are hustling.

• You'll need a publicist to promote and market your film.

• Las Vegas casinos will give you 1,000 to 1 odds that you'll fly back home with a check in your pocket.

Festivals may still be worth considering for the following reasons:

• Who knows—you may get lucky and sell your film.

• You'll get to premiere your film before audiences that are passionate about films.

• You may get the film reviewed in the local newspaper or even as part of a wrap-up report in one of the major publications.

• You'll get some valuable tips from other attendees.

• The seminars and panel discussions can be educational.

• There are fun parties to attend.

• Festivals offer an excellent opportunity to network.

• Having your film accepted by a festival is prestigious.

The publicist. To get maximum benefits at the festival, you'll need a publicist to set up appointments, pitch your film, and publicize it. It's a big job. In their excellent book, *The Complete Filmmaker's Guide to Film Festivals*, Rona Edwards and Monika Skerbelis write that, "Not only do you need to prepare your film for its screening, you need to publicize it. You can't just show your film and be done with it. You need to network, promote, and try and create heat so that the industry insiders attending the festival will take notice." The publicist will write press releases, try and get the film reviewed locally, set up radio and TV interviews, prepare press kits, handle special events, and host the screenings. Without a good publicist pitching your film, success at the festival will be greatly diminished.

General Tips:

• Make your appointments in advance. Most festivals will provide you with a list of attendees.

• Make sure your film is listed on IMDb.

• Your film's website should be current and include a trailer.

• If your film is not totally complete and quality checked, don't show it.

• Avoid showing your film in advance of the festival opening, but it's okay to give links to your film and/or your trailer after the opening when enthusiasm will be at its peak.

• Pick the right festival for your film. Check the types of films the festival screened in previous years. Talk to the festival programmer.

Withoutabox. A very useful time and money saver for filmmakers. Their website offers filmmakers an opportunity to scan over 5,000 film festivals from around the world and to submit films to 800 participating festivals. Films can be submitted online. No need to make hundreds of DVD screeners. Withoutabox is a subsidiary of IMDb (which, in turn, is a subsidiary of Amazon), so your film will also be automatically included with these services. Filmmakers just pay the published entry fee for each festival. Withoutabox makes its money charging the festivals.

These are the major film festivals, by calendar dates:

SUNDANCE FILM FESTIVAL (JANUARY)
Sundance Institute
5900 Wilshire Boulevard
Suite 800
Los Angeles, CA 90036
www.sundance.org

BERLIN INTERNATIONAL FILM FESTIVAL (FEBRUARY)
Potsdamer Strasse 5
10785 Berlin, Germany
www.berlinale.de

SOUTH BY SOUTHWEST FILM FESTIVAL (MARCH)
PO Box 685289
Austin, TX 78768
www.sxsw.com/film

TRIBECA FILM FESTIVAL (APRIL)
Tribeca Cinema
54 Varick Street
New York, NY 10013
www.tribecafilmfestival.org

SAN FRANCISCO INTERNATIONAL FILM FESTIVAL (APRIL)
39 Mesa Street
Suite 110/The Presideo
San Francisco, CA 94129
www.sffs.org

SEATTLE INTERNATIONAL FILM FESTIVAL (MAY)
305 Harrison Street
Seattle, WA 98109
www.seattlefilm.org

CANNES INTERNATIONAL FILM FESTIVAL (MAY)
3 Rue Amelle
75007 Paris, France
www.festival-cannes.org

LOS ANGELES FILM FESTIVAL (JUNE)
9911 W. Pico Boulevard
Los Angeles, CA 90035
www.lafilmfest.com

VENICE INTERNATIONAL FILM FESTIVAL (AUGUST)
La Biennal Di Venzia
Ca' Giustiniun
San Marco 1364/A
30124, Venice, Italy
www.labiennale.org

NEW YORK FILM FESTIVAL (SEPTEMBER)
The Film Society of Lincoln Center
70 Lincoln Center Plaza
New York, NY 10023
www.filmlinc.com

TORONTO INTERNATIONAL FILM FESTIVAL
350 King Street West
Toronto ON M5V 3X5, Canada
www.tiffg.ca

Important Festivals for Documentaries (listed alphabetically). Dates often change. E-mail for information:

AFI DOCS
8633 Colesville Road
Silver Spring, MD 20910
info@afidocs.com

BIG SKY DOCUMENTARY FILM FESTIVAL
113 W. Front Street
Suite 203
Missoula, MT 59802
news@bigskyfilm.org

DOCNYC
174 West 4th Street
Suite 180
New York, NY 10014
emilie@norget.com

HOT DOCS
110 Spadina Avenue
Suite 333
Toronto M5V 2K4, Canada
info@hotdocs.ca

FULL FRAME DOCUMENTARY FILM FESTIVAL
320 Blackwell Street
Suite 101
Durham, NC 27701
info@fullframefest.org

INTERNATIONAL DOCUMENTARY FILM FESTIVAL AMSTERDAM
Frederiksplein 52
1017 XN, Amsterdam, Netherlands
info@idfa.nl

Contact for the Human Rights Film Network (HRFN):

Human Rights Film Network
℅ Movies That Matter Foundation
Postbus 1968
1000 BZ Amsterdam, The Netherlands
www.humanrightsfilmnetwork.org

GAY FILM FESTIVALS:

OUT FEST
3470 Wilshire Boulevard
Suite 935
Los Angeles, CA 90010
outfest@outfest.org

MIAMI GAY AND LESBIAN FILM FESTIVAL
P.O. Box 530280
Miami, FL 33153
www.mglff.com

THREE DOLLAR BILL CINEMA FESTIVAL
1122 E. Pike Street
Suite 1313
Seattle, WA 98122
threedollarbillcinema.org

Chapter 21
Major Film Markets—Buyers and Sellers Wheeling and Dealing

> "No art passes our conscience in the way film does, and goes directly to our feelings, deep down into the dark rooms of our souls."
>
> —Ingmar Bergman

Film markets are totally different from film festivals. It's the reason I address them in a separate chapter in this book. In the publication *The Independent*, journalist Minhae Shim wrote that "At film markets the focus is on commerce. The goal of attending is to make production and distribution deals." Film festivals attract many people who simply love to see movies, rub shoulders with celebrities, and to drink and be merry. Attendees at film markets are all business. They are buyers and sellers focused entirely on making a deal. You do not attend a film market to party and have fun.

You should consider the following before you decide to attend a film market.

• They are usually more expensive than attending film festivals, some running as high as five figures.

• Negotiations are time-consuming, so you should schedule more time at the market than you would attending a festival.

• In addition to a publicist (which you'll need attending a festival), you will also need to hire an international sales agent. More about this below.

• The film market is a much more global event than a festival. Make sure you have trailers subtitled in different languages. Of the major markets listed below, only two take place in the US.

• At a film market, many buyers are willing to screen "work-in-progress" films.

International Sales Agent. Do not attend a film market without securing the services of an international sales agent for the following reasons:

• They have relationships with the major buyers. Without these relationships, cultivated over many years, the possibilities of selling your film are nil.

• They understand the global markets and the markets that will be suitable for your film.

• They often have a booth or a hospitality suite where they can pitch your film, together with the other films they represent.

• Your film has a better chance of being sold if it can be part of a package with several other films.

• They employ people who can speak several languages.

• They know how to negotiate a film deal.

• They will schedule appointments.

Lastly, if you make a deal, you will need an entertainment lawyer to review the agreement.

These are the **big three** film markets:

MARCHE DU FILM (MAY). It runs in conjunction with the Cannes Film Festival. It's regarded by many as the most important event in the industry and the leading meeting place for 3,200 producers, 2,300 exhibitors, 1,500 sales agents, and 790 festival programmers. They provide a "Pocket Guide" to help you navigate the many events taking place at the market. www.marchedufilm.com/en/lemarche

EUROPEAN FILM MARKET (FEBRUARY). It runs in conjunction with the Berlin International Film Festival (Berlinale). Last year, it attracted 8,396 participants. 107 nationalities were represented, 1,499 buyers, and 487 exhibitors. www.efm-berlinale.de/en/about-efm/facts-figures.html

AMERICAN FILM MARKET (AFM) (NOVEMBER). A stand-alone market not connected with any festival. A bit smaller than the two markets above, the AFM focuses more on US films. More importantly, this is a market friendlier to low-budget independent films and documentaries. 8,000 people attended last year from 70 different countries. www.americanfilmmarket.com/about-afm

You should also consider these smaller, more specialized film markets:

NATPE/MIAMI (JANUARY). This is the major US market serving the worldwide television community. Attending will be TV station groups, broadcast networks, cable/satellite networks, and executives handling Internet and home entertainment platforms. www.natpe.com/market

MIPCOM (OCTOBER). A shorter, five-day market in Cannes. Attending are the key decision makers in the TV and audio-visual content industry. www.mipcom.com/en/the-event

MIPTV (APRIL). Precedes the Cannes International Film Festival. MIPTV is the world's most established TV and digital content market and the biggest gathering of entertainment industry professionals. 100 countries were represented last year. www.mipcom.com

HONG KONG INTERNATIONAL FILM & TV MARKET (MARCH). Asia's largest film and entertainment market. In addition to film, the market also offers help in such diverse fields as designing games, production and post-production services, shooting locations, insurance, and film financing. www.hktdc.com/fair/hkfilmart-en/Hong-Kong-International-Film--TV-Market--FILMART-.html

CINEMART (JANUARY). Held in Rotterdam, CineMart is an unusual market in that attendance is by invitation only, and, if you are accepted, it's free. There are a few rules: the film should be new, minimum of 60 minutes, should have potential to be seen in international markets, and not been screened in another festival. The market includes the "Rotterdam Lab," which is a five-day training workshop for young and emerging filmmakers. www.iffr.com/professionals/CineMart/project_entry/

Chapter 22
Qualifying for an Oscar—Why Not?

"There's nothing quite like the idea of failing spectacularly to excite a filmmaker."

—Mike Figgis

Winning an Oscar, or even getting an Oscar nomination, can be as thrilling as winning the lottery. More importantly, your film will be recognized worldwide as being a bona fide winner. Your chances of landing a distributor and generating meaningful digital and online sales will be greatly improved. In other words, you've become a celebrity.

However, before you take the plunge, you must consider the following:

1. It's costly. You have to make multiple copies of your film for the Academy, and you'll have to book or rent a theater in New York and Los Angeles.

2. Getting nominated is unlikely. Last year, 150 documentaries were submitted. The Academy selected 15 films for what they call the short list. So the odds of just getting on the short list are 10 to 1. This list is then whittled down to the five nominees from which the winner will emerge. Now the odds get even longer. A casino gambler will probably tell you to get lost.

But, you are a passionate filmmaker, not a gambler, so you decide to go for it.

Documentaries have a slightly better chance. A feature film will be competing against the big Hollywood studios, so unless the feature film is supported by one of the major indie distributors, like Weinstein or Fox Searchlight, it stands very little chance of getting a nomination.

Requirements for Documentaries:

• A one-week run in an approved theater in New York (Manhattan only) and in an approved theater in Los Angeles. This is the toughest requirement for indie filmmakers who are self-distributing. It may require four-walling one or both theaters.

• The film must be reviewed in New York (*The New York Times*, *Time Out New York*, or the *Village Voice*) or in Los Angeles (*Los Angeles Times* or the *LA Weekly*). Reviews from television critics are not acceptable.

• The film must be projected in either 35mm, 70mm, or DCP.

• The film must have a minimum of four shows per day. The first show cannot begin before noon and the last show cannot begin after 10:00 p.m.

• An ad must be placed the week of the opening in the approved publications in New York and Los Angeles. The size must not be smaller than 1 inch x 2 inches.

- A minimum of 300 DVDs must be included in the submission package. Filmmakers who make the short list must submit two 35 mm or 70 mm film prints or two hard drives.

- The film must have a running time of more than 40 minutes.

- The film must be available for viewing by the general public with a box office admission price.

The Academy defines a documentary as a "theatrically released motion picture dealing creatively with cultural, historical, social, scientific, economic, or other subjects. It may be photographed in actual occurrence, or may employ partial reenactment, stock footage, stills, animation, stop-motion, or other techniques, as long as the emphasis is on fact and not fiction. Excluded from consideration are episodes extracted from a larger series, segments taken from a single composite program, and alternate versions of ineligible works."

Films that, in any version, receive a nontheatrical public exhibition or distribution before their first qualifying release will not be eligible for consideration. This includes broadcast and cable television, PPV/VOD, DVD distribution, and digital transmissions.

Unfortunately, the voting can become a popularity contest. Each voting member of the Docu Branch of the Academy (there are 175 members) must screen approximately 150 submissions. Most members have full-time jobs and have limited time to do much screening. It's quite possible that many members choose to screen only well-know films and/or films dealing with subjects that interest them.

Requirements for Short Subject Films:

• The film must be shorter than 40 minutes.

• The film only needs to run in one city: either New York (Manhattan) or Los Angeles. A theatrical run can be avoided altogether if the film won a qualifying award at a competitive film festival, as specified in the Documentary Short Subject Qualifying Festival List, or if the film won a Gold, Silver, or Bronze medal in the Academy's Student Academy Awards competition (Documentary Category).

• Only one show per day is required. The show cannot begin before noon or start after 10:00 p.m.

• A minimum of 50 DVDs must be included in the submission package. Filmmakers nominated must submit either two 35 mm or 70 mm prints or two DCP hard drives.

• All other requirements for full-length documentaries apply to short documentaries.

Requirements for Animated Films:

• An animated film is defined by the Academy as one in which the "movement and characters' performances are created using a frame-by-frame technique."

• Animation must figure in no less than 75% of the picture's running time.

• All other requirements for full-length documentaries apply to animated films.

Academy contact. The rules are long and complicated. Best to check with the Academy before you lift a finger:

Tom Oyer
The Academy of Motion Picture Arts and Sciences
8949 Wilshire Boulevard
Beverly Hills, CA 90211-1907
310-247-3000 x 1138
toyer@oscars.org

Chapter 23
Trade Publications—Read Them

"Read, read, read…if you don't read, you will never be a filmmaker."

—Werner Herzog

My first job, shortly after college, was as a broker trainee at the Wall Street firm of Oppenheimer & Co. The founder, Max Oppenheimer, was still around. At the conclusion of our training program, Mr. Oppenheimer addressed the trainees, imparting the usual words of wisdom. He concluded by asking us a very direct question: "What do you have to know to succeed in this business?" After observing blank stares from most us, he leaned forward so we wouldn't miss a word of his answer: "Know everything."

Schmoozing with fellow filmmakers at parties and festivals is surely the fun way to gather information. But, if you're a serious filmmaker, you'll want to subscribe to as many trade publications as you can afford. Before listing the major publications, a few notes:

• Subscription rates listed can change without notice.

• Check if the publication has a digital version. It will often cost less.

• If the publication is being shipped either to or from a foreign country, the cost will be higher.

- Compare the subscription price quoted by the publication with the prices quoted by Amazon and MagazineLine (www.magazineline.com). They may be considerably less.

- Google the publication to get more detailed information about the type of stuff covered.

- The rates quoted are for one-year subscriptions. Most publications will have a reduced rate if you subscribe for more than one year.

- All rates are quoted in US dollars.

Consider subscribing to the following publications:

VARIETY
11175 Santa Monica Boulevard
Los Angeles, CA 90025
1-323-617-9100
www.variety.com

The "bible" of the film industry. There's a weekly, daily, and online edition. VARIETY is noteworthy for covering late-breaking news, reviews, box office results, cover stories, and articles by well-informed journalists. $199.00 (48 issues).

THE HOLLYWOOD REPORTER
5700 Wilshire Boulevard
Suite 500
Los Angeles, CA 90036
1-323-525-2090
www.thr.com

This publication features longer articles including profiles of entertainment figures, interviews, articles about major releases, reviews, film festival previews, and an analysis of global business trends. $199.00 (51 issues).

MOVIEMAKER
2525 Michigan Avenue
Building #1
Santa Monica, CA 90404
310-828-8388
www.moviemaker.com

Includes a lively mix of interviews, trend-setting stories, DIY techniques, coverage of major festivals, distribution and financing tips. $14.95 (5 issues).

FILMMAKER
℅ Synapse Connect
225 High Ridge Road
East Building
Stamford, CT 06905
1-800-773-3142
www.filmmaker-the-magazine-of-independendent-film.com

This magazine offers timely advice and information to independent filmmakers. Past articles have dealt with directing, screenwriting, film financing, and an evaluation of film equipment. $18.00 (4 issues).

INDIEWIRE
665 Broadway
Suite 700
New York, NY 10012
917-289-7000
www.indiewire.com

It's free, so there's absolutely no reason not to subscribe. It's strictly an online daily publication that features late-breaking news, articles, and discussions of current film issues and events.

BOX OFFICE
60 Broad Street
Suite 3502
New York, NY 10004
1-818-286-3108
www.boxoffice.com

The magazine focuses on the exhibition business. It covers new theater openings, theater equipment, and profiles of successful theater operators. $49.95 (12 issues).

FILM COMMENT
Film Society of Lincoln Center
70 Lincoln Center Plaza
New York, NY 10023
1-888-313-6085
www.filmcomment.com

Published by the Film Society of Lincoln Center, it was awarded the "Best Arts Coverage" by *The Utne Reader*. For over 50 years it has featured a mix of essays, interviews, coverage of major festivals, and reviews. $29.95 (6 issues).

AMERICAN CINEMATOGRAPHER
The American Society of Cinematographers
1782 N. Orange Drive
Hollywood, CA 90028
1-800-448-0145
www.american_cinematographer.com

This publication focuses on the art and the craft of cinematography. It has included articles on domestic and foreign productions, television productions, and short films. It also features discussions on the latest film equipment and technologies. $16.99 (6 issues).

CINEAST
708 Third Avenue
5th Floor
New York, N.Y. 10017
www.cineast.com

Offers social, political, and esthetic perspectives on the cinema. $24.00 (4 issues).

I would also recommend buying these excellent books, all available on Amazon:

Filmmaking by Jason J. Tomaric

Think Outside: The Ultimate Guide to Film Distribution and

Marketing for the Digital Era by Jon Reiss

The Insider's Guide to Independent Film Distribution by Stacey Parks

The Digital Filmmaking Handbook by Sonja Schenk and Ben Long

The Complete Guide to Film Festivals by Rona Edwards and Monika Skerbelis

The Independent Film Producer's Survival Guide by Gunnar Erickson, Harris Tulchin, and Mark Hallopran

Independent Feature Film Production by Gregory Goodell

The Pocket Lawyer for Filmmakers by Thomas A. Crowell, Esq.

The Producer's Business Handbook by John J. Lee, Jr. and Anne Marie Gillen

Filmmaking for Dummies by Bryan Michael Stoller

Chapter 24
Film Equipment—Don't Overspend

"People never forget two things: their first love and the money they wasted watching a bad movie."

—Amit Kalantri

It may seem peculiar to include a chapter on film equipment in a book about film marketing, but the cost of buying or renting equipment will be a major expense in your overall budget. The less you spend on equipment, the more you can spend marketing your film. I also included this chapter because I've seen so many filmmakers overspend buying equipment. I've seen a growing compulsion on their part to buy the latest and the fanciest gadgets. It will be your vision and your talent that will determine the success of your film—not the equipment.

As recently as five years ago, the cost of professional film equipment and stock was the major obstacle to making an indie film. With the development of quality camcorders and, more importantly, digital cameras, the cost for making a quality feature-length film is within reach for even the most impecunious filmmaker. And the final technological breakthrough was the development of inexpensive post-production software. Instead of spending long and costly hours editing and splicing film, filmmakers can edit in minutes with the right software and computer. One of the most popular courses at NYU's film school teaches students how to make quality, feature-length films with a cell phone.

I have found the following sources very helpful:

Tom Barrance
Film Technology
www.learnaboutfilm.com
tom@learnaboutfilm.com

B&H-THE PROFESSIONAL SOURCE
www.bhphotovideo.com
askbh@BandH.com

A few notes:

• The prices quoted are subject to change without notice. I include the suggested list price, but most items can be purchased at a discount.

• You can spend more if your budget allows. I would not recommend spending less.

• I listed one item in each category in order to make it less overwhelming. The price for the item listed will give you a general idea of what you should spend if you prefer buying a different brand or model.

• If you're planning on producing one film, compare the costs of buying versus renting equipment.

• I focus on the four main pieces of equipment: the camera, sound equipment, lighting equipment, and post-production software. Without a doubt, you'll need more stuff. But these are the basics.

The Camera:

Panasonic AG-HMC80 3MOS AVCCAM HD Shoulder-Mount Camcorder. $1,699.00. This camera features solid-state DV recording, XLR inputs, and an ENG form factor to the high-definition imaging capability of the popular AG-HMC40. The progressive 3MOS image sensors record full HD images with an effective motion picture resolution of 2.51 MP. The camera also includes a new HD lens, 12x optical, 10x digital zoom, Optical Image Stabilization (OIS), dynamic range stretch, ability to produce high-quality 10.6 digital stills, large capacity SDHC memory card, three DV screen sizes, 2.7" wide-screen EVF/LCD monitor, manual focus ring, XLR line microphone input, and an HDMI output terminal. Unless your hand is steady as a rock, you'll also need to purchase an inexpensive tripod.

Sound Equipment:

Panasonic AG-MC200G Super-Directional Camera-Mountable Shotgun. $349.99. The sound is as important as the picture. Unless you are making a silent film, you should focus on producing good sound. People can see an indie film that looks washed-out on the screen and dismiss it as being artsy. But, if the sound is lousy, people will think the film is lousy. The Panasonic equipment listed has an XLR input that will allow you to plug in an external mic. This will enable you to get the mic away from the camera and closer to the actors.

Lighting Equipment:

VidPro Varicolor 312-Bulb Video and Photo LED Light Kit. $198.00. Best to buy a lighting set with LED bulbs. LED "arrays"

are good for producing even, soft lighting. The VidPro offers the following features: 5600-3200K color selector by dial, 100-10% brightness dimmer, snap-on diffuser, magnetic filter system, adjustable ball mount, and a rugged nylon carrying case.
Tip: For enhancing natural light, get a cheap reflector that includes a diffuser (to reduce and soften light), gold, white, and silver reflectors (for filling shadows), and a reflector with a black side to use as a "flag" (to block out light).

Post-Production Software:

Adobe Photoshop Elements 13 & Premiere Elements 13 for Mac and Windows. $89.00. The software combines two versatile and intuitive editing and organizational programs. This will help you to manage a complete digital imaging video workflow. A complete set of tagging controls, based on location or event, will enable you to navigate an immense catalog of imagery.

Tom Barrance, the technology wiz, offers this sage advice: "Don't get obsessed with having the latest filmmaking gear. Artists don't waste time worrying that they're using last year's pencils, and that great camera you bought a few months ago hasn't become worthless because there's a new that just came out."

Chapter 25
Terms & Definitions

> "It's incredible to see the creativity, beauty, and hardships people capture when filmmaking is opened up and shared with the world."
>
> —Jehane Noujaim

Advanced Television Systems Committee (ATSC). Replaced the NTSC. Sets the standard for high-definition images at 16:9 images and up to 1920 x 1080 pixels.

Aggregator Sometimes called the distributor. This is the person between the filmmaker and the digital platforms and/or cable-TV stations. The aggregator encodes the film and handles the submissions to the various outlets.

Alliance of Motion Picture and Television Producers (AMPTP) A trade association that is involved in negotiating guild and union contracts.

American Film Market (AFM) The major market in the US for buyers and sellers of film.

Ancillary Rights Covers all non-theatrical rights like DVD sales, the digital platforms, TV, and cable.

Back End The profit earned after all expenses have been deducted.

Blu-Ray A high-definition DVD.

Cable TV Television content that is transmitted by coaxial cable.

Cap The maximum amount a company can charge for expenses.

Completion Bond Insurance that guarantees investors and/or producers that a film will be completed by a certain date.

Day-and-Date Opening in multiple venues at the same time. Usually refers to a film opening in a theater while simultaneously being available on one of the digital platforms or on cable.

Digital Cinema Package (DCP). Digital projection of a film with a minimum resolution of 2048 x 1080 pixels.

Direct DVD/Digital Bypassing a theatrical run and going right to DVD sales, or transmitting the films on the digital platforms.

Directors Guild of America (DGA) A trade union representing film directors.

DIY Stands for do-it-yourself. Commonly used expression with filmmakers who self-distribute.

Electronic Sell-Through (EST) After paying a fee, viewers own the film by downloading it on a hard drive.

Errors and Omissions An insurance policy that protects a company from lawsuits and damages.

Exclusive Video On Demand (EVOD) A cable station offering video content on an exclusive basis.

Floor The amount an exhibitor deducts to cover expenses before giving the filmmaker/distributor a percentage of the box office income.

Four-Wall The rental of a theater for a set price for a set period of time.

Free Video On Demand (FVOD) A video streaming service offered at no charge and usually includes advertising before the film plays.

Guarantee A sum paid by an exhibitor regardless of the income generated at the box office.

House Nut Same as Floor. See above.

Indemnify A promise to protect someone or a company from loss or damage. Usually covered by Errors and Omissions Insurance (see above).

Independent Film and Television Alliance (IFTA) The trade organization primarily involved in international distribution.

Jumpstart Our Business Startups (JOBS) Legislation easing the rules for small businesses seeking investment capital.

Move Over Moving a film from one theater to another in the same market area.

Motion Picture Association of America (MPAA) The major trade association for the film industry. Known primarily for rating films.

National Association of Theater Owners (NATO) Major trade association representing theater owners.

National Television Standards Committee (NTSC) Sets the standard format for analog broadcasting. Replaced by ATSC. See above.

Negative Pickup The sale of all film rights.

Net Deal The distributor deducts all costs and collects all fees before making any payments.

Ninety/Ten Deal After deducting the house nut (see above), the exhibitor pays the filmmaker/distributor 90% of the box office income.

One Sheet Usually refers to the film poster.

Out Clause A clause in an agreement allowing a party to rescind for non-performance.

P&A The cost for prints and advertising.

Pay-Per View A one-time payment to view a film on cable TV.

Phase Alternation Line (PAL) The analog display standard that is predominant in areas outside the US.

Platform Digital companies that stream films, like iTunes, Netflix, Amazon, and Hulu.

Points The percentage of the profits offered to investors.

Pre-Sale Selling rights to a film prior to completion.

Press Kit A package usually compiled by the film's publicist containing comprehensive information about the film.

Producer's Rep A filmmaker's well-connected representative assisting in the selling and/or booking the film around the world.

Quality Control (QC) Requirements digital platforms set for film submissions.

Residuals Payment for each re-run after the initial showing.

Sales Rep Same as Producer's Rep. (See above.)

Screen Actors Guild (SAG) A trade union representing actors.

Streaming The transmission of a film from a digital company directly to the viewer's TV screen.

Self-Distribution A decision by filmmakers to handle distribution on their own.

Subscription Video On Demand (SVOD) A service in which a subscriber pays a set fee each month and is then allowed to view an unlimited number of films during that month.

Syndication Giving the rights, usually to a TV or cable station, to show re-runs of a TV series.

Trigger Clause A clause in an agreement indicating when payments will be made.

Transactional Video On Demand A video service in which viewers pay each time they screen a film.

Video On Demand (VOD) Films that can be ordered in advance and that are transmitted to a viewer's TV screen, computer, or mobile device.

Wide Release Distributing a film in multiple theaters simultaneously.

Writers Guild of America (WGA) The trade association representing writers.

INDEX

Academy of Motion Picture Arts and Sciences, 127
Adobe Software, 138
Adobe, 27
AFI DOCS, 116
Aggregator, 89
Alamo Drafthouse, 58
Amazon Instant Video, 73, 89
Amazon, 72, 90-91
American Cinematographer, 133
American Film Market (AFM), 121
American National Enterprises, 83
Americans for the Arts, 30
Apple iTunes, 64, 88
ATT U-Verse, 78

B & H- The Professional Source, 136
Barrance, Tom, 136
Beggs, Scott, 83
Belcourt Theater, 62
Berlin International Film Festival, 114
Bernfeld, Wendy, 64
Big Sky Documentary Film Festival, 116
Box Office Magazine, 132
Bright House Networks, 78
Broderick, Peter, 11

Cable Video On Demand (VOD), 77-81
Cablevision, 14, 78
Cannes International Film Festival, 115
Chozik, Amy, 79

Cineast, 133
Cinedigm, 81
Cinema Arts Cenre, 62
Cinema Village, 59
Cinemart, 122
Cinetic Media, 80
Circle Cinema, 62
City Cinemas, 58
Cleveland Cinematheque, 62
Closed Captioning, 89
Comcast, 14, 78
Complete Guide to Film Festivals, 134
Cox, 14, 78
CreateSpace, 73, 90
Creative Capital, 30
Crowdfunding, 29, 33-38
Crowell, Thomas A., 134

Digital Entertainment Group, 87
Digital Filmmaking Handbook, 134
DOC NYC, 116
Domain Name, 19
DVD Sales, 71-75

Edwards, Rona, 112
Elinor Bunin Munroe Film Center, 61
Equipment, Film, 135-138
Erickson, Gunnar, 134
Errors and Omissions Insurance, 68
European Film Market, 121

Facebook, 14, 21, 93-96
Film Buffs, 80

Film Comment, 132
Film Forum, 61
Film Independent, 30
Film Office, 32
Filmmaker, 131
Filmmaking for Dummies, 134
Ford Foundation, 31
Foundation Directory Online, 30
Full Frame Documentary Film Festival, 116

Gallagher, Nolan, 79
Gene Siskel Film Center, 61
Gillen, Anne Marie, 134
Golden Trailer Awards, 110
Goodell, Gregory, 134
Google AdWords, 97-102
Google, 14
Google, Organic Listing, 100
Grant Space, 30
Grants, 29, 30
GrantSelect, 30
Gravitas Releasing, 79, 80
Gray, Tim, 87
Grove, Elliott, 13

Hallopran, Mark, 134
Hollywood Reporter, 130
Hong Kong International Film & TV Market, 122
HOT DOCS, 116
Houston Cinema Arts Festival, 61
HTML5, 27
Hulu Plus, 77, 89
Human Rights Film Network, 117

Independent Feature Film Production
Independent Film Producer's Survival Guide, 134
Indiegogo, 35
IndieWire, 132
International Documentary Film Festival (Amsterdam), 117
International Sales Agents, 120
Internet Movie Database (IMDb), 23-27
iReach, 47
iTunes, See Apple iTunes

Jacob Burns Film Center, 61
JOBS Act, 38

Kapipal, 36
Keywords, 98
Kickstarter, 35

Laemmle Theaters, 58
Landmark Theaters, 56
Lee, John J., 134
Lincolm Plaza, 59
LinkedIn, 103-106
Litwak, Mark, 64
LiveLeak, 27
Long, Ben, 134
Los Angeles Film Festival, 115

Marche Du Film, 121
Marketing for the Digital Era, 134
McGurk, Chris, 81
Mediacom, 78
Merin, Jennifer, 107

Metacritic, 23
Metascore, 23
Miami Beach Cinematheque, 60
Miami Gay and Lesbian Film Festival, 117
Micheaux, Oscar, 83
MIPCOM, 122
MIPTV, 122
Moviemaker Magazine, 131
Movies of Delray, 60
MPAA, 24, 63
Music Box Theater, 60

NATPE (Miami), 121
Netflix, 14, 64, 71, 77, 88
New Beverly Cinema, 59
New York Film Festival, 115
Newswire LLC, 47

Oscar Qualifying, 123-127
OUT FEST, 117

Pacific Theaters, 57
Panasonic Cameras, 137
Pay-Per-1,000 Impressions, 105
Pay-Per-Click (PPC), 93, 103, 105
Pocket Lawyer for Filmmakers, 134
PR Newswire, 47
Producer's Business Handbook, 134
Prudential Foundation, 31
PRWeb, 47

Quad Cinema, 59
Quality Control Report (QC), 51

Raindance Film Festival, 13
Rasmuson Foundation, 31
Reading International, 57
Reiss, Jon, 134
Rockefeller Foundation, 31
RocketHub, 36
Roxie Theater, 60

San Francisco International Film Festival, 114
Schenk, Sonja, 134
Seattle International Film Festival, 115
Securities and Exchange Commission (SEC), 38
Shim, Minhae, 119
Skerbelis, Monika, 112
Sloss, John, 80
South By Southwest Film Festival, 114
State Tax Credite, 31
Stetler, Brian, 79
Stewart, Joan, 43
Stoller, Bryan Michael, 134
Streaming, 87-92
Subtitles, 91
Sudderlink Communications, 78
Sundance Cinemas, 57
Sundance Film Festival, 114
SUNN Classic Pictures, 84

Terms & Definitions, 139-144
Three Dollar Bill Cinema Festival, 117
Time Warner, 14, 78
Toronto International Film Festival, 115
Trailers, 107-110

Tribeca Film Festival, 114
Tulchin, Harris, 134
Twitter, 14, 21

United States Artists, 31

VARIETY, 130
Venice International Film Festival, 115
Verizon, 78
VHX, 64
VidPro Light Kits, 137
Vimeo, 27
Vimeo, 27, 64

Website Host, 19
Withoutabox, 113
Wordpress, 19

Yahoo, 14
YouTube, 27
YouTube, 27, 64

www.ingramcontent.com/pod-product-compliance
Lightning Source LLC
Chambersburg PA
CBHW022134080426
42734CB00006B/364